# PuzzleMania®
## Numbers, Please!

HIGHLIGHTS PRESS

*Honesdale, Pennsylvania*

# CONTENTS

When you finish a puzzle, check it off √.
Good luck, and happy puzzling!

## Hidden Pictures®

## It's Logical

## Number Games

# Calculate It

# A-Mazing!

# Get Into Shapes

# ...ck the Code

# Time and Money

# Words Count

# Super Challenge

# Leaping Lemurs

The lemurs that live in these trees have a rule. When they are finished, every row of trees across, down, and diagonally will have **30** lemurs. We've written the correct number on some trees. Use this information to figure out how many lemurs belong on the others. Write the correct number on each tree.

16

12

8

4

# What's for Dessert?

The **Puzzlemania Diner** is famous for its desserts. In addition to being delicious, these menu items are code crackers! Each coded space has two numbers. The first number tells you which menu item to look at; the second number tells you which letter in that item to use. For example, the first coded letter is **1–3**. The **1** tells you to go to **PEACH PIE**. Count **3 letters** in, and you've got an **A**. Fill in the rest to find some sweet jokes.

6

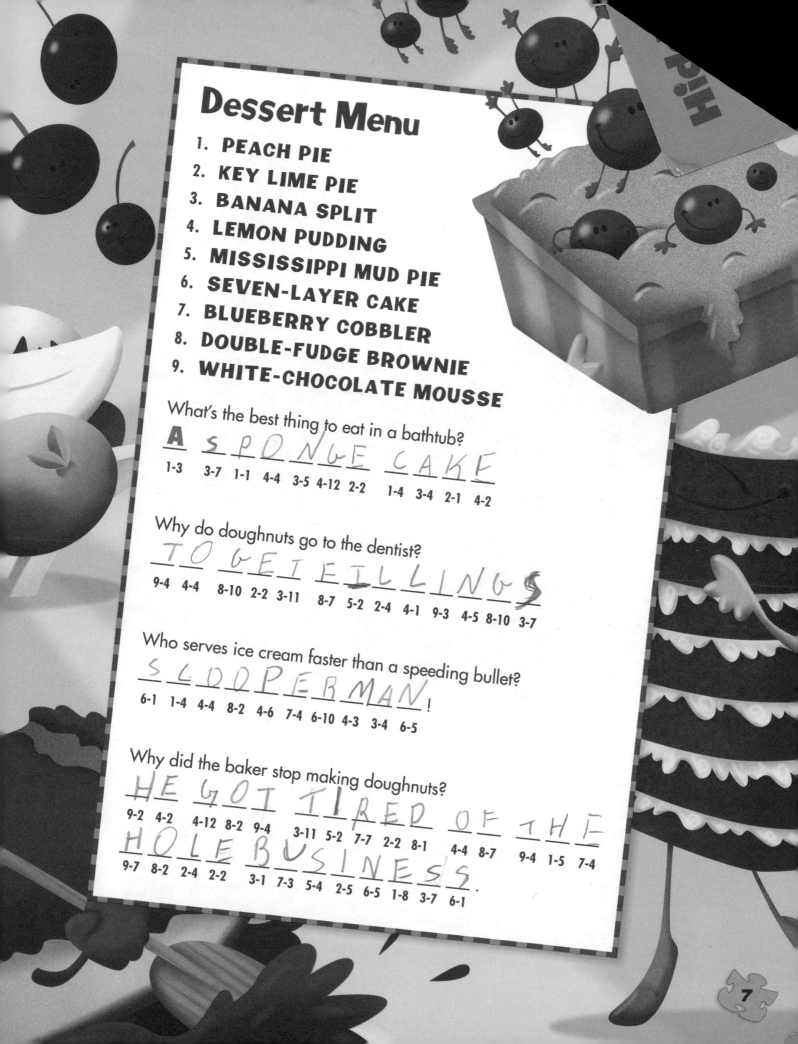

# Dessert Menu

1. PEACH PIE
2. KEY LIME PIE
3. BANANA SPLIT
4. LEMON PUDDING
5. MISSISSIPPI MUD PIE
6. SEVEN-LAYER CAKE
7. BLUEBERRY COBBLER
8. DOUBLE-FUDGE BROWNIE
9. WHITE-CHOCOLATE MOUSSE

What's the best thing to eat in a bathtub?

**A** S P O N G E   C A K E
1-3  3-7 1-1 4-4 3-5 4-12 2-2   1-4 3-4 2-1 4-2

Why do doughnuts go to the dentist?

T O   G E T   F I L L I N G S
9-4 4-4  8-10 2-2 3-11  8-7 5-2 2-4 4-1 9-3 4-5 8-10 3-7

Who serves ice cream faster than a speeding bullet?

S C O O P E R M A N !
6-1 1-4 4-4 8-2 4-6 7-4 6-10 4-3 3-4 6-5

Why did the baker stop making doughnuts?

HE  GOT  TIRED  OF  THE
9-2 4-2  4-12 8-2 9-4  3-11 5-2 7-7 2-2 8-1  4-4 8-7  9-4 1-5 7-4
HOLE  BUSINESS.
9-7 8-2 2-4 2-2  3-1 7-3 5-4 2-5 6-5 1-8 3-7 6-1

Illustrated by Brian White

**There is more than meets the eye at this aquarium. Can you find each hidden shape?**

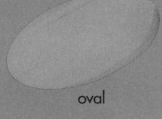
oval

arrow

cross

circle

hexagon

diamond

heart

square

star

moon

pentagon

triangle

parallelogram

rectangle

trapezoid

# Add It Up

To find your way through this maze, add the first pair of numbers (**6+5**).
Draw a line to the answer (**11**), then move to the next pair of numbers
and do the same. Answers may be to the left, right, up, or down.

Start

| | | | | | | |
|---|---|---|---|---|---|---|
| 6+5 | **12** | 8+7 | **15** | 4+7 | **26** | 6+22 | **28** | 4+12 |

**11**    **14**    **13**    **25**    **16**

21+8   **29**   7+9   **17**   6+8   **14**   13+12   **21**   15+4

**26**    **16**    **36**    **23**    **19**

8+14   **24**   19+4   **25**   29+7   **34**   6+4   **25**   5+15

**22**    **23**    **13**    **14**    **20**

10+21   **33**   13+6   **19**   8+5   **12**   3+12   **30**   17+13

**31**    **17**    **15**    **15**    **32**

15+2   **28**   4+7   **6**   3+3   **26**   16+16   **13**   3+7

**17**    **24**    **16**    **32**    **21**

6+3   **18**   11+2   **22**   9+1   **10**   17+7   **24**   Finish

10

# Order in the Court!

This judge needs some order in her courtroom. You can help by figuring out what number comes next in each series. Hurry, before she has to pound her gavel again!

**A.** 1, 8, 15, 22, _29_

**B.** 36, 30, 24, 18, _____

**C.** 64, 32, 16, 8, _____

**D.** 3, 9, 27, _____

**E.** 4, 17, 30, 43, _____

**F.** 81, 72, 63, _____

**G.** 256, 64, 16, _____

**H.** 5, 25, 125, _____

**I.** 12, 34, 56, _____

**J.** 1, 4, 9, 16, _____

**K.** 2, 12, 20, 21, 22, _____

**L.** 12, 6, 18, 12, 24, _____

**M.** 12, 23, 34, 45, _____

**N.** 3, 6, 33, 36, 63, _____

**O.** 20, 25, 22, 27, 24, _____

**P.** 9, 36, 12, 48, _____

**Q.** 9, 6, 12, 9, 15, _____

**R.** 40, 10, 60, 15, _____

Illustrated by Jim Paillot

11

# Zero Money

Nyle and Nadia are headed for the Numberville Candy Store, where they can use zeroes as money. Solve the equations along the correct path and see how many zeroes they can pick up. **Only the zeroes in the answers count as money.** How many lollipops can they buy?

1,000

$10 \div 5 =$

$500 - 1 =$

$85 + 25 =$

Numberville

$50 - 40 =$

$25 + 25 =$

$100 + 100 =$

$100 \times 0 =$

$100 - 100 =$

Illustrated by Nathan Jarvis

### Bank of Zeroes

Keep track of your zeroes! Write the answers to the equations here, then count how many zeroes you picked up.

# Ship Shapes

This ship is 800 feet long from stem to stern and 400 feet wide from port to starboard. It's up to you to figure out what it weighs. To find the answer, look at the shapes in the code. Count how

14

many times you see each shape on and around the ship. Then find the letter in the blue box that matches that number and write it in the correct blank. If you find all the shapes, you'll find your answer!

**What does the ship weigh?**

I T  W E I G H S

A C C H G R.

Illustrated by Terry Kovalcik

15

# Thanksgiving Tidbits

Marielle and Kelson are helping their mom bake an apple pie to bring to Grandma's. But first they have to buy the ingredients. Look at the recipe on the sign and find all the items on it. How much money will all the ingredients cost?

**APPLE PIE**
1 bag of sugar
1 bag of flour
cinnamon
nutmeg
1 bag of apples
butter

# Pyramid Puzzles

**D**o you notice anything interesting about the numbers in the first pyramid? See if you can fill in the numbers missing from the other two pyramids. Hint: See how the columns in each pyramid add up.

**Pyramid 1**

```
                  1
              3   3   6
          2   4   4   1   5
      7   4   1   1   3   1   5
  10  3   4   2   1   0   4   5   10
```

**Pyramid 2**

```
                  9
              6   2   1
         29  17   8   2   10
      16  __   3   5   1   10  29
  30  14   1   4   6   26  10   1   30
```

**Pyramid 3**

```
                  19
             16   6   5
         13  __   4   __  14
     18  23  18   7   15  28  16
  37  29  __   4  __   5   10  __  __
59  __  __ 11   4   3   9  __  30  30  __
```

17

# Clock Comedy

Time for a joke! Each clock shows a different time. You can use them to find the answer to a riddle. Write each clock's letter in the space that has a matching digital time. Hurry, there isn't a second to lose!

D

H

K

A

E

I

T

O

N

C

## Why was the clock so lonely?

<u>I</u> __ __ __ __ __ __ __ __ __
12:00 8:00  5:00 9:45 2:30  6:30 10:50 10:50 6:30 7:45

__ __  __ __ __ __  __ __ .
8:00 10:50  8:00 10:50 3:15 4:05  8:00 10:50

18

Illustrated by Jim Steck

# One OF a KiNd

Here's one puzzle you won't want to miss. Twenty words that contain the letters *ONE* are hidden in the grid. Look for them up, down, across, backwards, and diagonally. There's just one catch. For each word, the letters *ONE* have been replaced by the number **1**. For example, BALONEY appears as BAL**1**Y. If you can find every one, you're number one in our book!

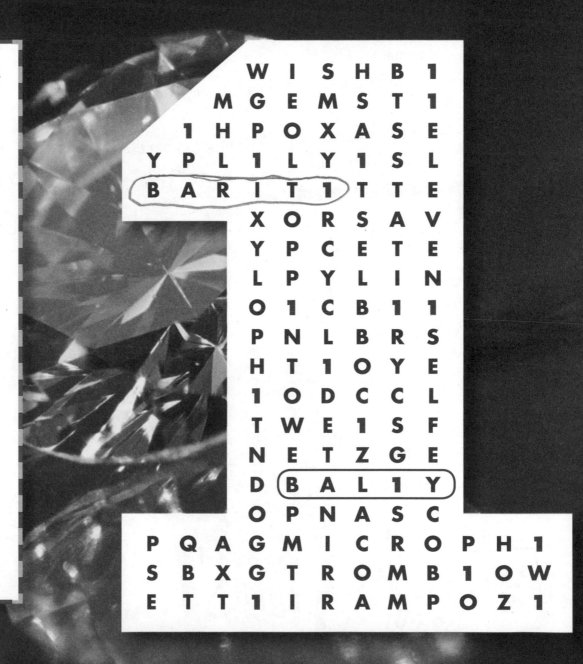

## Word List

- ~~BALoneY~~
- ~~BARITone~~
- CALZone
- COBBLESTone
- COLoneL
- CYCLone
- DOGGone
- GEMSTone
- LoneLY
- MARIoneTTE
- MICROPHone
- MoneY
- oneSELF
- OPPoneNT
- OZone
- SAXOPHone
- STATIoneRY
- TROMBone
- WISHBone
- XYLOPHone

```
W  I  S  H  B  1
M  G  E  M  S  T  1
1  H  P  O  X  A  S  E
Y  P  L  1  L  Y  1  S  L
B  A  R  I  T  1  T  T  E
   X  O  R  S  A  V  E
   Y  P  C  E  T  E
   L  P  Y  L  I  N
   O  1  C  B  1  1
   P  N  L  B  R  S
   H  T  1  O  Y  E
   1  O  D  C  C  L
   T  W  E  1  S  F
   N  E  T  Z  G  E
   D  B  A  L  1  Y
   O  P  N  A  S  C
P  Q  A  G  M  I  C  R  O  P  H  1
S  B  X  G  T  R  O  M  B  1  O  W
E  T  T  1  I  R  A  M  P  O  Z  1
```

19

# Floral Arrangements

Mr. Vidalia sells six different types of flowers. Each kind costs a different amount per flower ($.50, $.75, $1.00, $1.25, $2.00, and $2.50). Look

**CLUES**

1. Roses are the most expensive flowers.
2. The cheapest flowers go in bin C.
3. Chrysanthemums go between the lilies and the tulips.
4. Daisies cost $1.00 each. They go directly above the lilies.
5. The $2.00 flowers belong directly below the carnations.
6. The flowers that cost 75 cents go in bin E. Daisies go in bin A.

Illustrated by Scott Peck

at the clues and figure out where each flower should be located on the cart and how much each kind should cost. Hint: Start with clue number 6.

A $ Flower:

B $ Flower:

C $ Flower:

D $ Flower:

E $ Flower:

F $ Flower:

# Five Sides

Fitz's favorite number is five, and he has just finished drawing a maze with five sides. Help him get out of this perplexing pentagon, and when you're done, see if you can spot five sets of five things in this scene.

START

FINISH

Illustrated by Susan Miller

22

# Baking Day

arrowhead

car

pennant

mushroom

candle

boot

sock

banana

dart

ring

cowbell

shuttlecock

ladder

slice of pizza

23

# Ancient Auction

The amazing explorer R. K. Ologest found these artifacts while digging in Africa last year. Several museums have placed bids as shown on the chart. Circle *true* or *false* after each statement, and write the corresponding letter in the blanks.

Illustrated by Michael Austin

| OBJECTS | MONTH FOUND | BIDS | | |
| --- | --- | --- | --- | --- |
| | | This Stonian Museum | Museum of Unnatural Stuff | Vannegie Institute |
| Painted vase | February | $11,700 | $10,900 | $12,200 |
| Stone hammer | August | $500 | $1,500 | $1,900 |
| Wooden wheel | July | $46,800 | $61,000 | $64,000 |
| Animal-skin shoe | March | $14,750 | $13,000 | $9,800 |
| Stone bowl | September | $4,900 | $6,900 | $4,600 |
| Leather pouch | September | $14,000 | $15,500 | $18,560 |
| Bone necklace | April | $48,100 | $31,200 | $31,000 |

1. The highest price offered for the stone bowl is less than the lowest price offered for the bone necklace. TRUE: H  FALSE: N

2. If all the items are sold for the highest bids offered, the total will be $166,410. TRUE: Y  FALSE: O

3. The Vannegie Institute offers the highest bids on everything. TRUE: L  FALSE: S

4. This Stonian Museum has the winning bid on only one item. TRUE: A  FALSE: T

5. Based on the bids, the wooden wheel is the item the museums believe is the most valuable. TRUE: E  FALSE: I

6. The museum willing to spend the greatest sum of money for all the objects is This Stonian Museum. TRUE: B  FALSE: R

7. The object whose bid prices are the closest is the painted vase. TRUE: I  FALSE: A

8. The painted vase is the first object Mr. Ologest found. TRUE: C  FALSE: Y

**What do you call a very, very, very old joke?**

Pre- __ __ __ __ __ __ __ __
       1  2  3  4  5  6  7  8

# Digit Does It!

Inspector Digit just received a package of items from an investigator working on a postal forgery case. Unfortunately, a breeze blew everything off the inspector's desk. You can help recover

Illustrated by John Nez

the evidence if you decipher the investigator's message. Hint: The first line reads, "Dear Inspector Digit."

# Animal Airlift

The flood waters are up on the Watchout River. The helicopter that came to rescue these animals can only hold up to 1,000 pounds at a time. For example, the helicopter cannot take the elephant and the hippopotamus together in one trip

SUPER CHALLENGE

325 pounds

80 pounds

95 pounds

800 pounds

550 pounds

46 pounds

130 pounds

Illustrated by Scott Peck

because they weigh too much when flown together. Can you figure out the fewest number of trips needed to move all the animals to a safe location? Hint: Start by finding two animals whose weight equals 1,000 pounds.

300 pounds

20 pounds

350 pounds

675 pounds

600 pounds

THE ANIMAL ASSOCIATION

29

# One, DoS, Three

The numbers one through ten appear here in both Spanish and English. Each will fit into the grid in only one way. Use the number of letters as a clue to where each might fit. We've filled in the first "one" to get you started. When you have filled the grid, write the letters in the red boxes in order from top to bottom in the spaces below to see the Spanish word for 100. *Good luck! ¡Buena suerte!*

| ENGLISH | SPANISH |
| --- | --- |
| ~~One~~ | Uno |
| Two | Dos |
| Three | Tres |
| Four | Cuatro |
| Five | Cinco |
| Six | Seis |
| Seven | Siete |
| Eight | Ocho |
| Nine | Nueve |
| Ten | Diez |

O N E

The Spanish word for 100 is ☐☐☐☐☐☐ .

Rocky, Rudy, and Ronnie are running in a **5-mile race** today to raise money for a local charity. Rocky ran at a speed of 5 miles per hour. Rudy ran at a rate of 10 minutes per mile. And Ronnie finished the race in 45 minutes. Who ran the fastest? Hint: Figure out how many minutes it took each to finish the race.

# Play by the Book

Rachel, Eduardo, Abby, and Daniel started a book club. They meet every Saturday in the park. Each friend likes a different kind of book, and each reaches the park in a different way. From the clues, can you figure out how each person gets to the park and what kind of book each likes to read?

Use the chart to keep track of your answers. Put an **X** in each box that can't be true and an **O** in boxes that match.

| | Science Fiction | Mystery | Adventure | Humor | Scooter | Walking | Bike | Skateboard |
|---|---|---|---|---|---|---|---|---|
| **Rachel** | | | | | | | | |
| **Eduardo** | | | | | | | | |
| **Abby** | | | | | | | | |
| **Daniel** | | | | | | | | |

1. Rachel is older than Eduardo, but younger than Daniel, who is not the oldest.

2. The boy who rides his bike likes to read about aliens in the future.

3. One girl likes mysteries, while the older boy, who walks to the playground, laughs a lot while reading.

4. The oldest friend rides a scooter and doesn't like mysteries.

# Hopscotch Game

slice of
pizza

sailboat

envelope

teacup

balloon

crescent
moon

lightning
bolt

Illustrated by Tamara Petrosino

bell

slice of
lemon

comb
ruler

ice-cream bar
kite

candle

sock

33

# Witch Way

Wendy Witch is lost! Help her find the way back to her house. Once you've found the right path, solve the equations along that path. Write the answers, in order, in the blanks above Wendy's home. Then stick around and crack the code.

Start

$6 \div 2 =$

$4 \times 3 =$

$5 \div 5 =$

$7 + 3 =$

$8 - 5 =$

$9 \times 9 =$

$10 \div 2 =$

$5 \div 1 =$

$8 \times 7 =$

Illustrated by Becky Blake

$2 \times 1 =$

$9 \div 3 =$

$9 - 4 =$

$8 + 4 =$

$3 + 2 =$

# To Solve This Riddle, Crack the Code!

Have you solved the equations and filled in the blanks? Now you can answer the riddle! Find all the bats, black cats, cauldrons, and potion bottles in and around Wendy's house. Each represents a letter:

**bats: R   black cats: M   cauldrons: B   potion bottles: O**

Start with bats. How many can you find? Write an *R* in the blank that matches the number you found. Do that with the rest and you've solved the riddle!

What do you call two witches who live together? __ __ __ __ __ MATES

Write your equation answers here: __ __ __ __ __ __

$2 \times 1 =$

FINISH

$6 - 3 =$

# Alley-Oops

A

T

I

M

I

S

When did the bowler like to practice?

_____ _____   _____ _____ _____

_____ _____ _____ _____ _____   _____ _____ _____

# Party Path

Can you help Tasha find her way to the party? Start at the 9 in the top corner. You may move to a new box by **adding** 4 or by **subtracting** 5. Move up, down, left, or right.

| Start | 9 | 15 | 18 | 10 | 15 | 19 |
|-------|----|----|----|----|----|----|
| | 4 | 7 | 11 | 21 | 16 | 20 |
| | 8 | 12 | 15 | 5 | 12 | 15 |
| | 15 | 11 | 10 | 14 | 17 | 10 |
| | 12 | 17 | 6 | 9 | 13 | 14 |
| | 9 | 18 | 21 | 7 | 20 | 18 | Finish |

Illustrated by Peter Grosshauser

# Don't Stair

The stairway on the side of this old abandoned windmill has 30 steps. On the first step sits 1 pigeon. On the second step sit 2 pigeons. On the third step are 3 pigeons. This continues until the 30th step, where there are 30 pigeons. How fast can you discover how many pigeons there are altogether?

Illustrated by Michael Austin

# For a Change

The Ellensbury School held a fundraiser to buy new books. For a week, each class brought in coins and spare change. The amounts collected are on the jars. Can you tell which class collected the most money and which collected the most coins?

Miss Ellis
550 pennies
80 nickels
55 dimes
20 quarters

Mr. Ryan
634 pennies
30 nickels
25 dimes
36 quarters

Mrs. Macy
380 pennies
60 nickels
75 dimes
16 quarters

# Totally!

Gidget Digit loves to play with numbers. Just for fun, she put together these lists. See if you can figure out which list gives you the largest answer. When you've got that, write the colored letters from that list in order in the spaces below to find out the name of Gidget's pet hamster.

### 1

- NumBer of days in ApRil
- DivIded by the number of bears in the Goldilocks story
- Plus the number of leGs on a spider
- MInus the number of quarTers in a dollar

**TOTAL:** _____

### 2

- Number of voWels (not includIng Y)
- MultiplieD by the number of sides on a pentaGon
- Plus the number of dimEs in two dollars
- Divided by the number of points in a fooTball field goal

**TOTAL:** _____

### 3

- Number Of states in the USA
- Divided by the numbeR of singers in a duet
- Plus the numbeR of sides on a decagon
- MInus the number of hourS in a day

**TOTAL:** _____

**The name of Gidget's hamster is**

__ __ __ __ __ __ .

# Seaside Shapes

Count all the triangles and rectangles you see in this picture. Which shape is there more of?

Triangles _____

Rectangles _____

Illustrated by Paul Richer

42

43

# Roaming Rover

Rover, the robot dog, is programmed to find one of the objects here in the testing lab. Can you follow the directions to help Rover find the right object?

Start at the X.
Go south 5 spaces.
Go east 3 spaces.
Go north 2 spaces.
Go east 2 spaces.
Go south 5 spaces.
Go west 10 spaces.
Go north 5 spaces.
Go east 1 space.

Illustrated by R. Michael Palan

# To the Hoop

Player #8 is a star at tonight's game! He has scored **eleven** points so far. But he's only shot the ball **five** times. If he made it in the hoop each time, how many of each type of shot did he make? He scored at least one of each.

**FREE THROW = 1 POINT**

**BASKET = 2 POINTS**

**THREE-POINT BASKET = 3 POINTS**

Illustrated by Ken Spengler

45

cup

pliers

hand mirror

fishhook

handbell

sneaker

paper airplane

pennant

safety pin

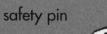

spoon

wristwatch

sailboat

# The 🔑 to It All

Illustrated by Scott Burroughs

**Dear Oscar,**

1. The office key is a primary color.

2. No key color has the same number of letters as the door it opens.

3. The green key does not open the shed.

4. The blue key opens either the front or the back door.

Oscar is taking care of his friend Irma's house while she is away on vacation. Irma left him a key chain and a note. Each key is a different color and opens a different door. From the clues on Irma's note, can you figure out which key is which?

Use the chart to keep track of your answers. Put an **X** in each box that can't be true and an **O** in boxes that match.

|  | Front | Back | Shed | Car | Office |
|---|---|---|---|---|---|
| **gold** |  |  |  |  |  |
| **blue** |  |  |  |  |  |
| **red** |  |  |  |  |  |
| **green** |  |  |  |  |  |
| **purple** |  |  |  |  |  |

# Watch the Difference

Each watch or clock below shows a time that's after noon but before midnight. First figure out the difference in time between each pair of timepieces. Write that time difference in the space

**3 hours** O

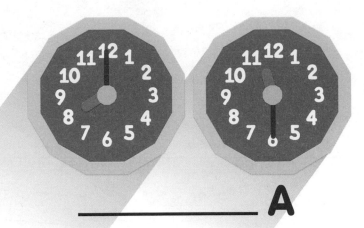

_____ A

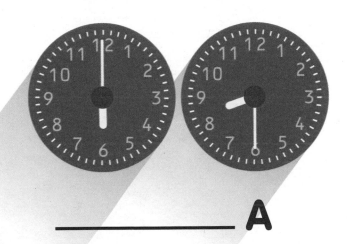

_____ A

_____ D

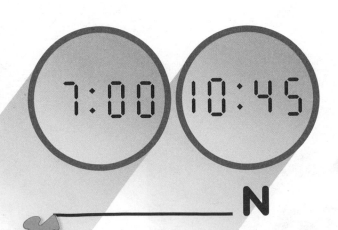

_____ N

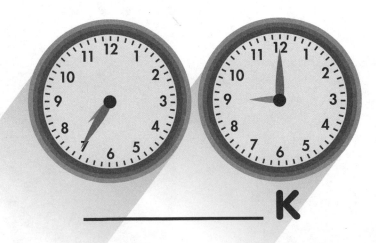

_____ K

48

underneath the pair. Arrange the times in order, from the smallest time difference to the greatest time difference. Once you have the order, write the letters near each clock into the blanks to answer the riddle. We did the first to get you started.

_____ **H**

_____ **N**

_____ **S**

_____ **O**

_____ **M**

 (digital clocks reading 5:15 and 5:55)

_____ **L**

 (digital clocks reading 4:55 and 5:45)

_____ **O**

**What did the digital clock say to its mother?**

" __ __ __ __, __ __!  __ __ __  __ __ __ __ __ __!"

49

# Ice-Cream Dreams

It sure is a hot day at Izzy's Ice-Cream Counter. Help Josh, Sammy, Michaela, and Neal sort out their change. Quick, before the ice cream melts!

Josh gave Izzy a $5 bill and got 80 cents in change. How much was his triple-scoop banana split sundae?

Michaela's and Neal's ice-cream cones cost $6.80 together. Michaela received $3.20 in change. How much money did she give Izzy?

Sammy spent $5.50 on her milkshake and has $2.40 left. How much did she start with?

Illustrated by Jennifer Zivoin

# Zig Zag Zig

Can you place the numbers 1 through 9 in the circles on this page? Every number should appear in one circle. It looks easy enough, but there is a catch. Every arrow must point to a circle containing a greater number.

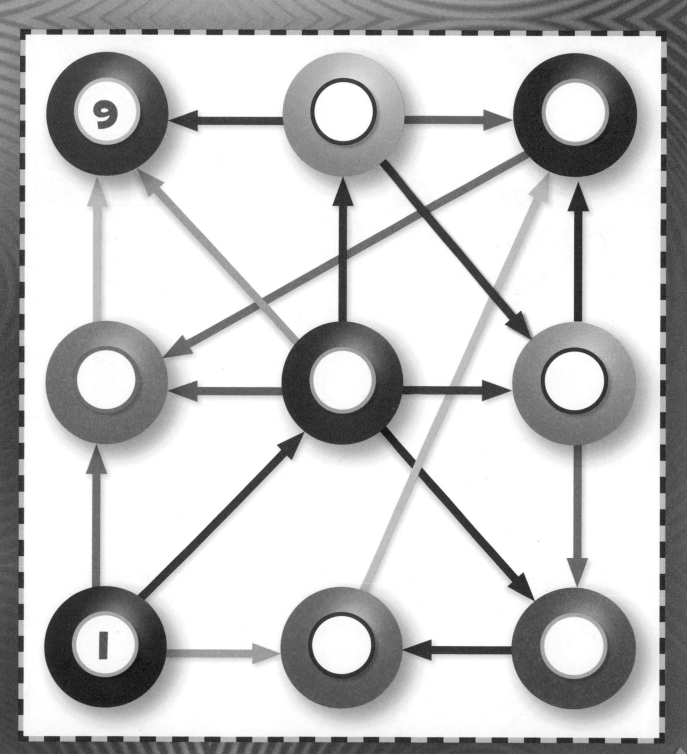

Illustrated by Hey Kids!

51

# Pattern Partners

Look at each pair of partners in the left column. Can you find the item in one of the columns, A, B, or C, that will pair with the pattern in the center?

**A**  **B**  **C**

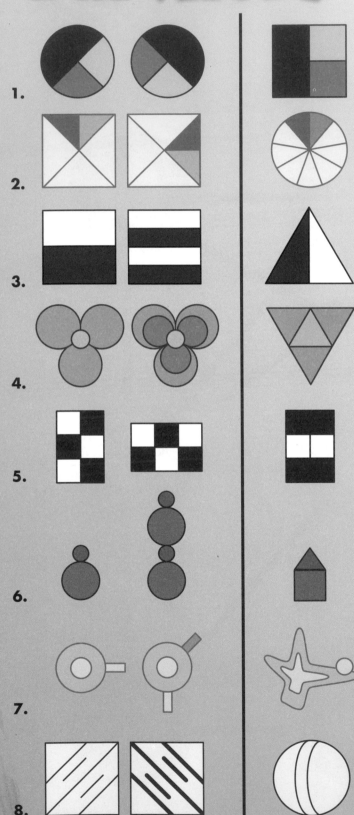
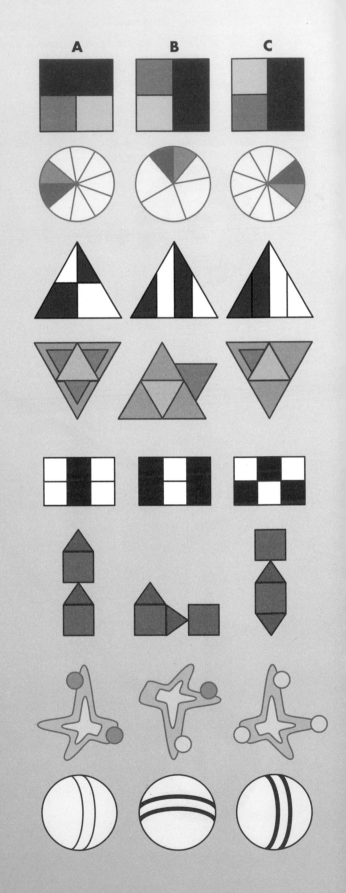

1.

2.

3.

4.

5.

6.

7.

8.

# Hidden Pictures®
# The King Wins

Illustrated by David Coulson

bird

boomerang

envelope

feather

hanger

kite

mug

book

baseball

piece of candy

comb

crescent moon

fish

lightning bolt

53

# Shell Search

Ashton, Lola, Aimee, and Cameron are racing to see who can pick up the most seashells. Follow each path to see where each person ends up. Then count the seashells to see who picked up the most.

Illustrated by Dan McGeehan

ASHTON

LOLA

AIMEE

CAMERON

55

# Truck Tunes

Use the number pairs to solve the riddle on this page. For the first number in each pairing, move right in the grid. For the second number in each pairing, move up in the grid. Write the letters you find in the correct spaces.

## What do long-distance truckers listen to?

○ ○ ○ ○ ○ - ○ ○ ○ ○ ○ ○ ○    ○ ○ ○ ○ ○

1,7  4,2  2,5  8,6  5,4    9,9  7,3  4,8  6,6  2,3  4,2  7,8    3,6  9,2  8,6  3,9  1,7

56

Illustrated by Garry Colby

# Minus Maze

To find your way through this maze, subtract the first pair of numbers (**16-11**). Draw a line to the answer (**5**), then move to the next pair of numbers and do the same. Answers may be to the left, right, up, or down.

Start

| | | | | | | | |
|---|---|---|---|---|---|---|---|
| 16-11 | 5 | 13-13 | 0 | 26-12 | 6 | 16-15 | 1 | 23-1 |

Illustrated by Hey Kids!

# Nothing To It

**3 LETTERS**

NIL
NIX
NON

**4 LETTERS**

GONE   HOLE   LOVE
NADA   NONE
NULL   VOID
ZERO

**5 LETTERS**

BLANK
EMPTY
LAPSE
NADIR

**6 LETTERS**

NAUGHT

**7 LETTERS**

~~NOTHING~~
SHUT OUT

**8 LETTERS**

GOOSE EGG
OMISSION

58

# Folding Fun

Each piece of paper here can be folded to make one of the objects on the shelves. Can you match each finished

Illustrated by Rocky Fuller

object with its flat diagram? All of the folds are shown. They're represented by the dotted lines on each piece of paper.

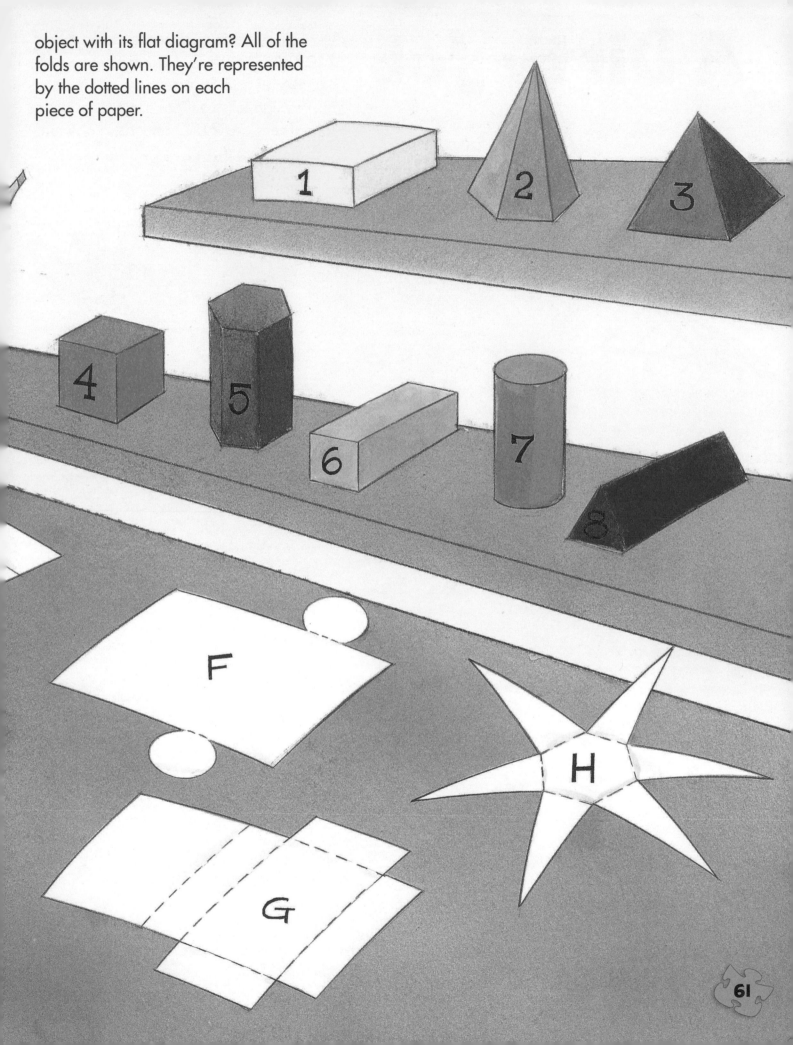

# A Dirty Job

Peter's pickup can transport a maximum of 750 pounds per trip. How many trips will it take for him to remove the entire pile? Hint: The sign tells us that Peter has to move 6 tons. There are 2,000 pounds in one ton.

CLEAN FILL 6 TONS

Illustrated by Michael Austin

# Batting Logic

The Puzzlemania Panthers have a new batting order this season. Can you help the team figure out who bats when? Use these clues to fill in the batting order on each player's card. Can you knock this one out of the ball park?

**Clues**

**A.** The kids wearing glasses do not bat 1st or 9th.

**B.** The boy with braces bats 1st.

**C.** The 8th and 9th batters have the same first initial.

**D.** The number on the jersey of the boy batting 2nd is twice as much as the number of the kid batting 4th.

**E.** Batter 6, a girl, has the same color hair as batter 7.

**F.** The girl outfielder bats 3rd.

SUPER CHALLENGE

**60**
**Lindsey**
**pitcher**

**22**
**Seth**
**center field**

**47**
**Cody**
**3rd base**

1

**55**
**Laura**
**1st base**

**10**
**Claudia**
**right field**

**44**
**Hector**
**catcher**

**35**
**Jacob**
**2nd base**

**29**
**Troy**
**left field**

**20**
**Ariel**
**shortstop**

Illustrated by Mike Moran

63

# Hidden Pictures® Professor Parrot

Illustrated by Arieh Zeldich

fish

vase

artist's brush

hedgehog

envelope

rabbit

teacup

needle

heart

ring

moth

pinecone

pen

boot

# Magic Maze

Tricky Trixie has gotten lost on her way to her big magic show. Can you help her find the right path to the stage before her audience disappears? The symbols will tell you which way to move.

**Move 1 space DOWN**

**Move 1 space UP**

**Move 1 space RIGHT**

**Move 1 space LEFT**

| Path 1 | Path 2 | Path 3 | Path 4 | Path 5 | Path 6 |

Illustrated by Scott Burroughs

Can you look at each clock and figure out what time it's supposed to be? Once you figure out the times, read the letter on the sign near each clock in order from midnight to noon. The letters should tell you the new clockmaker's name.

T
:

I
:

C
:

**The new clockmaker's name is:**

,

____  ____  ____  ____  ____  ____  ____  ____  ____

# Toys for Twins

Nate and Jada want to buy presents for their younger twin brothers. They bought four toys from the store window and paid $13.20 with their allowance money. Which four toys did they buy?

$5.25

$7.50

$1.75

$3.25

500 PIECES!

Illustrated by Christine Schneider

$4.40

Magic Kit

$3.50

$4.20

$5.10

$2.00

# GOING UP!

Place the numbers **1** through **15** in these windows. The problem is that you cannot place consecutive numbers in windows next to each other. They cannot be touching above, below, or diagonally.

Illustrated by Jim Steck

# Similar Circles

All these circles have something in common, except for one circle. Can you tell which circle doesn't belong?

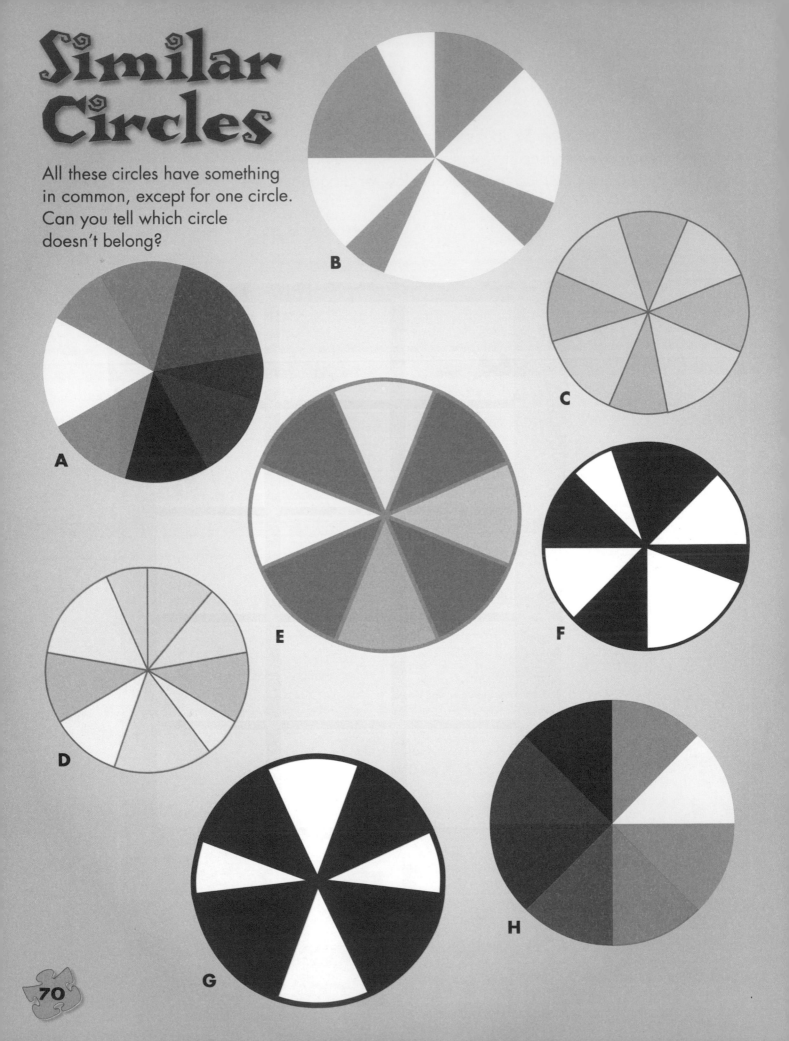

A

B

C

D

E

F

G

H

# A Head For Figures

Why is Danny standing on his head? He is looking for the one number that is the same when you read it upside down. Can you find the number that does not change when you turn the board upside down?

Illustrated by Jerry Zimmerman

# Three's a Crowd

Cross out all the boxes in which the number cannot be evenly divided by three. Then write the leftover letters in the spaces to spell the answer.

| 10 P | 12 T | 16 A | 33 H | 8 A | 22 S | 24 E | 11 G | 25 A | 13 T | 40 D |
|------|------|------|------|------|------|------|------|------|------|------|
| 15 B | 42 E | 20 L | 30 R | 60 M | 16 C | 18 U | 7 H | 44 S | 36 D | 54 A |
| 4 D | 21 T | 48 R | 14 Q | 57 I | 39 A | 35 S | 51 N | 45 G | 63 L | 27 E |

**Where did the Three Musketeers go on vacation?**

The BERMuDA Triangle

Illustrated by Steve Skelton

72

# Gone Fishing

Brooke and three friends went fish shopping at the pet store. From the clues below, can you figure out what color fish each friend got and what tank decoration each picked out?

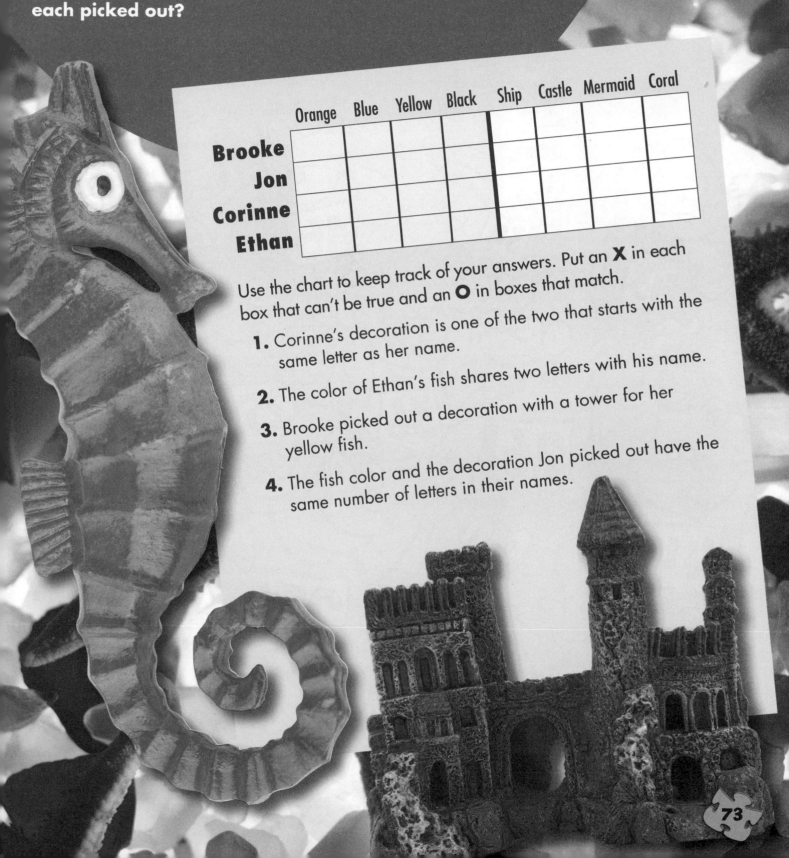

|          | Orange | Blue | Yellow | Black | Ship | Castle | Mermaid | Coral |
|----------|--------|------|--------|-------|------|--------|---------|-------|
| Brooke   |        |      |        |       |      |        |         |       |
| Jon      |        |      |        |       |      |        |         |       |
| Corinne  |        |      |        |       |      |        |         |       |
| Ethan    |        |      |        |       |      |        |         |       |

Use the chart to keep track of your answers. Put an **X** in each box that can't be true and an **O** in boxes that match.

1. Corinne's decoration is one of the two that starts with the same letter as her name.

2. The color of Ethan's fish shares two letters with his name.

3. Brooke picked out a decoration with a tower for her yellow fish.

4. The fish color and the decoration Jon picked out have the same number of letters in their names.

# Winning Number

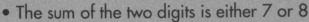

Somewhere in this picture is the winner of this year's Puzzlemania Marathon. Use these clues to figure out the number of the runner who won the race:

- The sum of the two digits is either 7 or 8
- If you switch the order of the digits, the new number would be 27 greater than it is now.

# Hidden Pictures®
## Piggy Problems

slice of watermelon

needle

fishhook

pennant

ring

toothbrush

light bulb

bell

leaf

Illustrated by Maxim Mitrofanov

pear

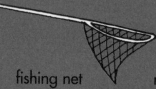
fishing net

musical note

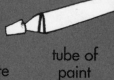
tube of paint

top hat

spoon

# Jungle Fun

Explorer Evie is hunting for the hidden treasure! **Three paths will take her there**, but she needs to pick up exactly **100 POINTS** along the way. Use the key to figure out which path will give her enough points to take her safely to the treasure chest.

**KEY**

Pile of coins = 15 points

Key = 20 points

BANANAS = 10 points

Bottle = 5 points

**START**

76

FINISH!

Illustrated by Larry Jones

77

# Money Maker

Shade in the square that contains the value of each of the following coin combinations The shaded squares should make sense once you are done.

4 dimes and 3 pennies
4 nickels and 6 pennies
2 quarters, 2 dimes, and 4 pennies
3 dimes, 1 nickel, and 2 pennies
1 quarter and 6 nickels
2 quarters and 13 pennies
3 quarters and 2 pennies
7 nickels
1 dime, 2 nickels, and 3 pennies
3 quarters and 2 nickels
1 quarter and 2 pennies
4 nickels and 4 pennies
2 quarters, 3 nickels, and 2 pennies
1 quarter and 4 dimes
2 quarters, 2 dimes, and 3 pennies
5 dimes and 3 pennies
6 dimes and 16 pennies
2 dimes and 1 nickel
9 nickels
1 dime and 1 nickel
3 quarters
3 dimes and 3 pennies

Illustrated by Scott Peck

# Lucky Pyramid

Can you make it to the top of the pyramid and recover the lost treasure? You'll need exactly 50 coins to claim it. Start at the bottom and work your way up. You can only move to a new stone if it is touching the stone you are currently on. Otherwise, you will slide to the bottom. Good luck!

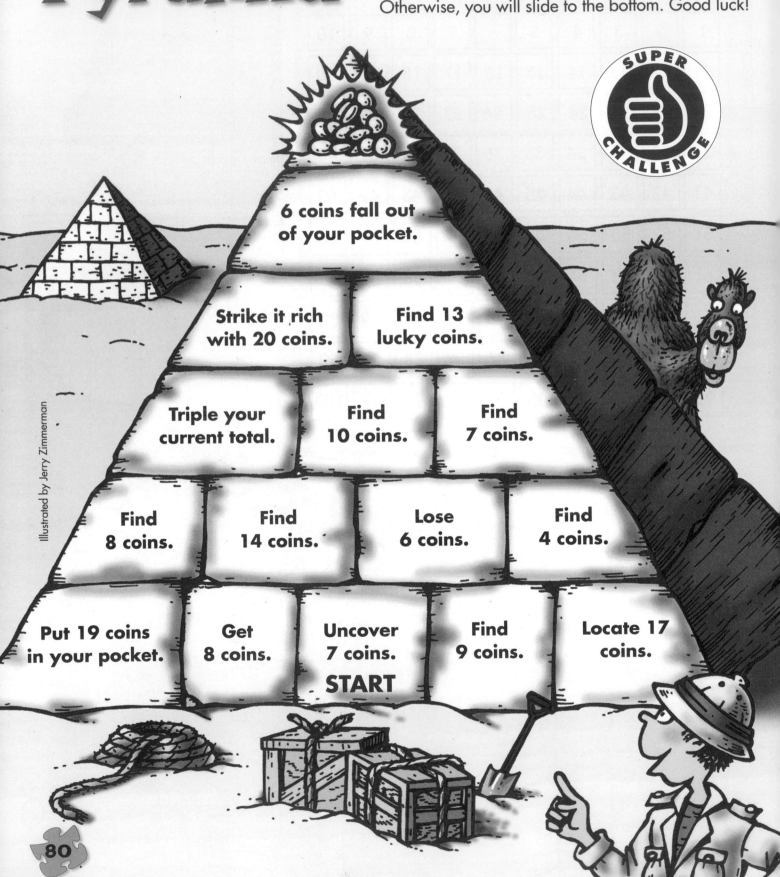

SUPER CHALLENGE

6 coins fall out of your pocket.

Strike it rich with 20 coins.

Find 13 lucky coins.

Triple your current total.

Find 10 coins.

Find 7 coins.

Find 8 coins.

Find 14 coins.

Lose 6 coins.

Find 4 coins.

Put 19 coins in your pocket.

Get 8 coins.

Uncover 7 coins.
**START**

Find 9 coins.

Locate 17 coins.

Illustrated by Jerry Zimmerman

80

# Hidden Pictures®
## Albert Einstein

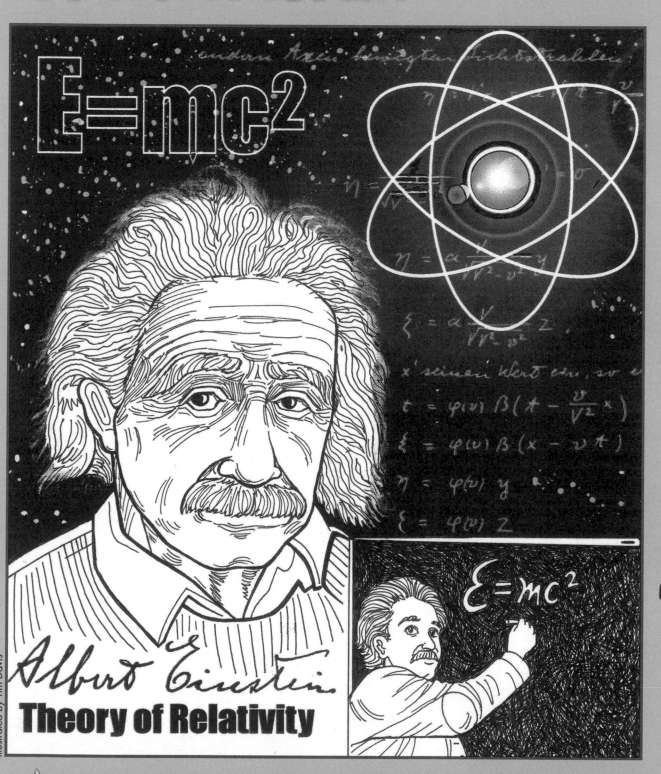

needle

bird

ice-cream cone

comb

shoe

toothbrush

snake

candle

ring

pencil

paper clip

sailboat

spoon

81

# One, Deux, Three

The numbers one through ten appear here in both English and French. Each will fit into the grid in only one way. Use the number of letters as a clue to where each might fit. We've filled in the first "one" to get you started. When you have filled the grid, write the shaded letters in order from top to bottom in the spaces below to see the French word for 100.

*Good luck! Bonne chance!*

| ENGLISH | FRENCH |
|---------|--------|
| ~~One~~ | Un |
| Two | Deux |
| Three | Trois |
| Four | Quatre |
| Five | Cinq |
| Six | Six |
| Seven | Sept |
| Eight | Huit |
| Nine | Neuf |
| Ten | Dix |

**The French word for 100 is**

☐☐☐☐ .

# For Good Measure

Mac and Mike have two trucks, and they need to load exactly four tons of gravel onto the train car. Once they've loaded any gravel on a truck, they cannot dump it back on the pile. Any extra weight will cause the train car to break. How can they do it?

Hint: Imagine filling the 3-ton truck with gravel, then pour that gravel into the 5-ton truck. Fill the 3-ton truck again. If you pour as much of that gravel into the 5-ton truck as you can, how much will be left in the 3-ton truck?

3 TONS

5 TONS

ROCKVILLE LINE

Illustrated by Scott Peck

# Game On!

Andrew and three of his friends entered a video game competition. From the clues below, can you figure out which game each friend played and which place he or she took?

Use the chart to keep track of your answers. Put an **X** in each box that can't be true and an **O** in boxes that match.

| | Space Traveler | Golf Guru | Race Car Fun | Zany Zoo | 1st | 2nd | 3rd | 4th |
|---|---|---|---|---|---|---|---|---|
| **Andrew** | | | | | | | | |
| **Briana** | | | | | | | | |
| **Cassie** | | | | | | | | |
| **Diego** | | | | | | | | |

1. One of the girls took 1st place in Zany Zoo.
2. Andrew's game had exactly 8 letters in its name.
3. Diego's place was ahead of Briana, but behind Andrew.
4. Briana played her favorite game, Race Car Fun.

# Math Mirth

The Math Club is holding its annual comedy night. Can you guess the answers to these riddles? All the letters you need are in the word list. Each fraction tells you which letters to use.

**1.** What is a math teacher's favorite dessert?

P _ _ _ _ _ _ _ _

First ⅓ of **PIG**
First ½ of **UMPIRE**
First ¾ of **KING**
First ⅓ of **PILLOW**

**2.** Which knight helped King Arthur build his round table?

S I _ _ _ _ _ _ _ _ _

First ⅔ of **SIT**
Last ⅔ of **ARC**
Last ½ of **PLUM**
First ½ of **FERRET**
Last ½ of **SENTENCE**

# Digit Does It!

Ring-a-ding Rosie, the bell burglar, has burgled another bell. While the Quasimodos were holding their annual Solstice Dance, Rosie broke in and took all the silver bells in Mr. Q's collection. She left a note

that may provide a clue to her whereabouts. Can you help Digit decipher the code and bell this crooked cat? The first line reads, "Dear Inspector Digit."

Dear Inspector Digit
20 19 23 7   15 11 6 9 19 21 5 10 7   20 15 17 15 5 '
sorr
6 10 7 7 1   5 10   7 15 11 17   23 11 20

7 4 11 .   15   16 23 3 19   22 15 17   22 15 13 13 '

5 16 19   22 15 17 17 19 6 5   22 19 13 13   15 11

5 16 19   21 10 13 13 19 21 5 15 10 11 '   22 4 5

15 3 19   13 19 18 5   9 13 19 11 5 1

22 19 16 15 11 20 .   15 18   1 10 4   21 10 4 11 5

5 16 19   10 5 16 19 7   22 19 13 13 6 '   1 10 4 13 13

14 11 10 2   2 16 23 5   7 10 10 12   5 10

7 15 11 17   12 19   4 9   15 11   23 5   5 16 19

22 19 13 3 19 20 19 7 19   16 10 5 19 13 .

# Treasure Hunt

Can you find a path to the buried treasure? Start at the **5** in the top corner. You may move to a new box by **adding** 5 or by **subtracting 3**. Move up, down, left, or right.

**Start**

| 5 | 10 | 17 | 10 | 7 | 12 |
|---|----|----|----|----|----|
| 5 | 7 | 12 | 13 | 4 | 9 |
| 11 | 6 | 9 | 8 | 21 | 18 |
| 16 | 19 | 6 | 11 | 16 | 15 |
| 13 | 18 | 20 | 12 | 21 | 12 |
| 10 | 15 | 17 | 15 | 20 | 17 |

**Finish**

# Diamondbacks

Draw four lines inside this diamond to make nine equal-sized diamonds.
*Hint: How do you draw a grid for a game of tic-tac-toe?*

Draw four lines inside this diamond to make eight equal-sized triangles.

Illustrated by David Helton

# Tricky Sticks

You'll have to "stick to it" if you want to solve these puzzles. For the first two, the toothpicks you need to move are marked in **red**. After that, you'll have to figure it out for yourself!

**1** Here are eight toothpicks. Can you make two boxes by moving just two?

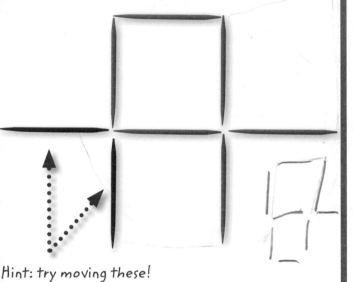

Hint: try moving these!

**2** These seven toothpicks make two triangles. Can you move two to make three triangles?

**3** Move just two toothpicks to turn this shape upside down.

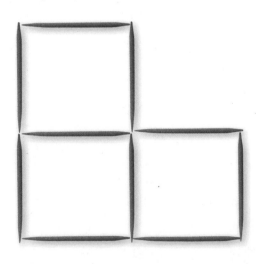

**4** Move two toothpicks so this house faces a different direction.

# Hidden Pictures
# Owlgebra

comb

cupcake

umbrella

bell

fish

sailboat

funnel

artist's brush

fishhook

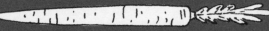
carrot

toothbrush

wristwatch

banana

teacup

Illustrated by Maxim Mitrofanov

91

# Show Time

Lena and three of her friends went to the multiplex movie theater. Each saw a different movie and bought a different snack. From the clues below, can you figure out what each person chose?

Use the chart to keep track of your answers. Put an **X** in each box that can't be true and an **O** in boxes that match.

| | Comedy | Drama | Action | Science Fiction | Popcorn | Taffy | Licorice | Chocolate Bar |
|---|---|---|---|---|---|---|---|---|
| **Lena** | | X | | | | | | |
| **Jack** | | | | | | O | | |
| **Ethan** | | | | | | | | |
| **Jasmine** | | | | O | | | | |

1. All the movies started at the same time, and the science-fiction film was the shortest.

2. The friend who saw the sci-fi movie ate licorice.

3. Jack laughed so hard at his movie, he didn't even finish his taffy.

4. Lena does not like drama or sweet snacks.

5. Jasmine was the first friend back to the lobby after her movie was over.

# Block Party

Can you tell which set of blocks was used to make each tower?

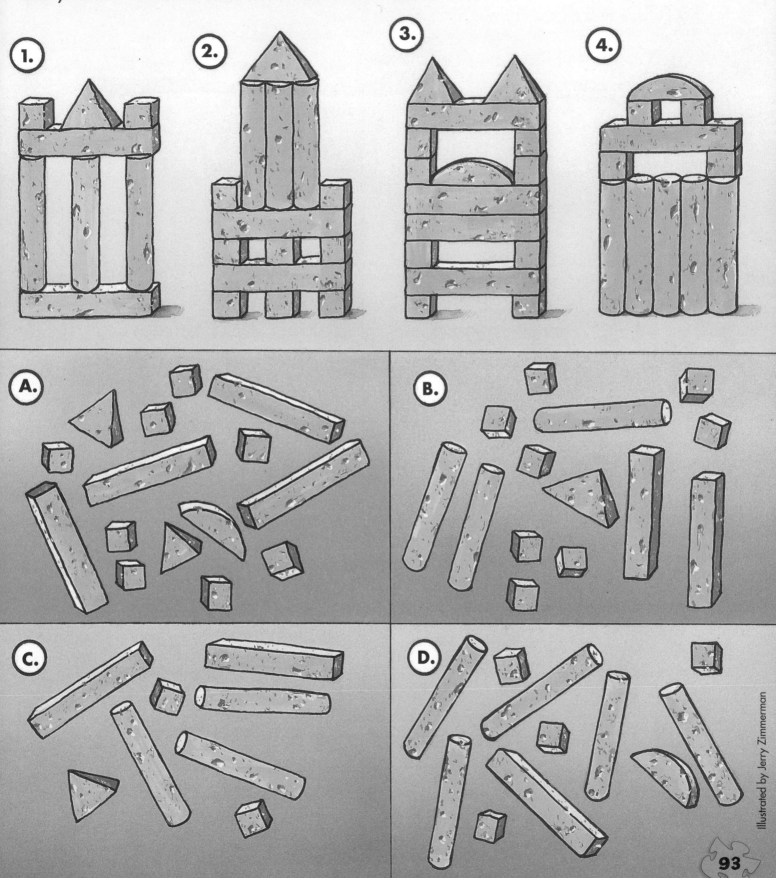

93

# Knock Three Times

Each clue in this puzzle has something to do with the number 3.
Read each clue and put the answer in the correct boxes.

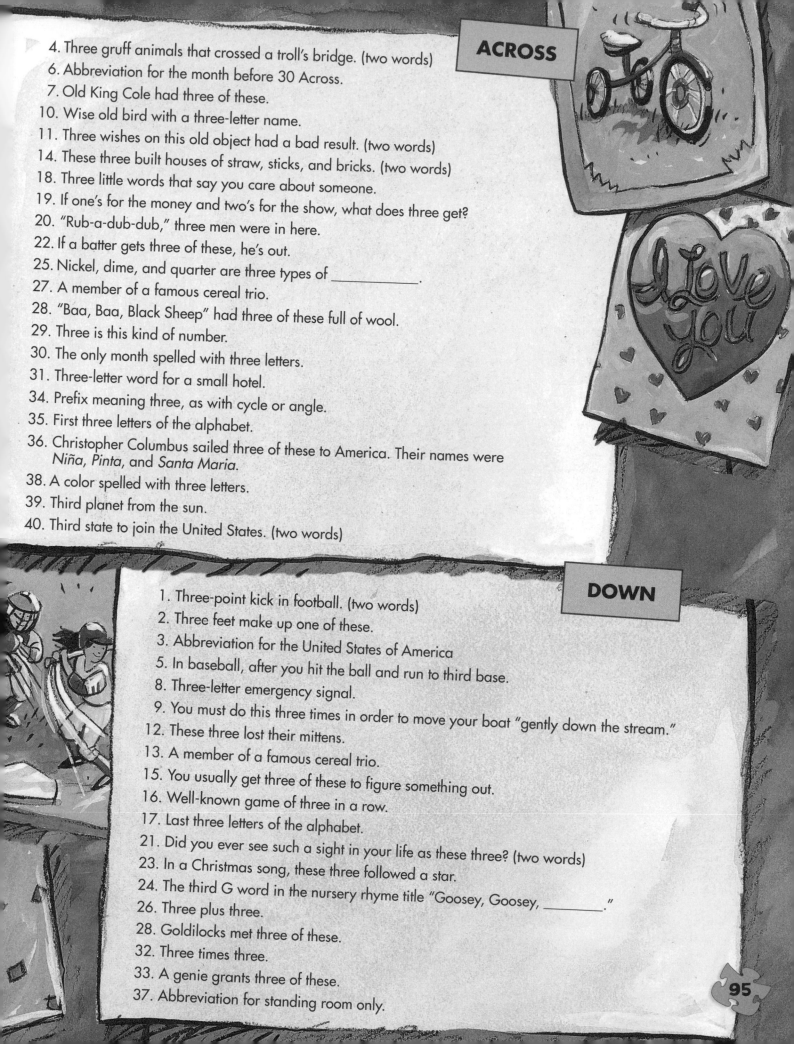

4. Three gruff animals that crossed a troll's bridge. (two words)
6. Abbreviation for the month before 30 Across.
7. Old King Cole had three of these.
10. Wise old bird with a three-letter name.
11. Three wishes on this old object had a bad result. (two words)
14. These three built houses of straw, sticks, and bricks. (two words)
18. Three little words that say you care about someone.
19. If one's for the money and two's for the show, what does three get?
20. "Rub-a-dub-dub," three men were in here.
22. If a batter gets three of these, he's out.
25. Nickel, dime, and quarter are three types of _____.
27. A member of a famous cereal trio.
28. "Baa, Baa, Black Sheep" had three of these full of wool.
29. Three is this kind of number.
30. The only month spelled with three letters.
31. Three-letter word for a small hotel.
34. Prefix meaning three, as with cycle or angle.
35. First three letters of the alphabet.
36. Christopher Columbus sailed three of these to America. Their names were *Niña*, *Pinta*, and *Santa Maria*.
38. A color spelled with three letters.
39. Third planet from the sun.
40. Third state to join the United States. (two words)

1. Three-point kick in football. (two words)
2. Three feet make up one of these.
3. Abbreviation for the United States of America
5. In baseball, after you hit the ball and run to third base.
8. Three-letter emergency signal.
9. You must do this three times in order to move your boat "gently down the stream."
12. These three lost their mittens.
13. A member of a famous cereal trio.
15. You usually get three of these to figure something out.
16. Well-known game of three in a row.
17. Last three letters of the alphabet.
21. Did you ever see such a sight in your life as these three? (two words)
23. In a Christmas song, these three followed a star.
24. The third G word in the nursery rhyme title "Goosey, Goosey, _____."
26. Three plus three.
28. Goldilocks met three of these.
32. Three times three.
33. A genie grants three of these.
37. Abbreviation for standing room only.

95

# Choosing Chores

Jared and Emilee do chores to earn some extra money.
Help them figure out how much money they've earned this week.

| Chore | Pay |
|---|---|
| Feed the Cats | 25¢ |
| Walk the Dog | 75¢ |
| Set the Table | 50¢ |
| Sweep the Floor | $1.00 |
| Take out the Trash | 50¢ |
| Dust your Bedroom | $1.25 |

Jared fed the cats twice a day for a week and set the table and swept the floor twice each. How much money has he made? Is that enough for him to buy a new game for $5.95?

Emilee wants to buy a new bracelet for $6.00. She has already dusted her room, set the table twice, and walked the dog three times. How many times does she have to take out the trash to earn enough money to buy the bracelet?

Illustrated by Kathryn Mitter

Spelling Bee
Champions

# PENNANT WINNERS

Flora, Phil, and Felix raised 15 flags up the flagpoles. Place the numbers 1 through 15 on the flags so that no two consecutive numbers are next to each other. They cannot be side by side, above and below, or diagonally. Numbers 1 and 15 are in place. Can you figure out the rest?

Illustrated by Jim Steck

97

# Sort Shirts

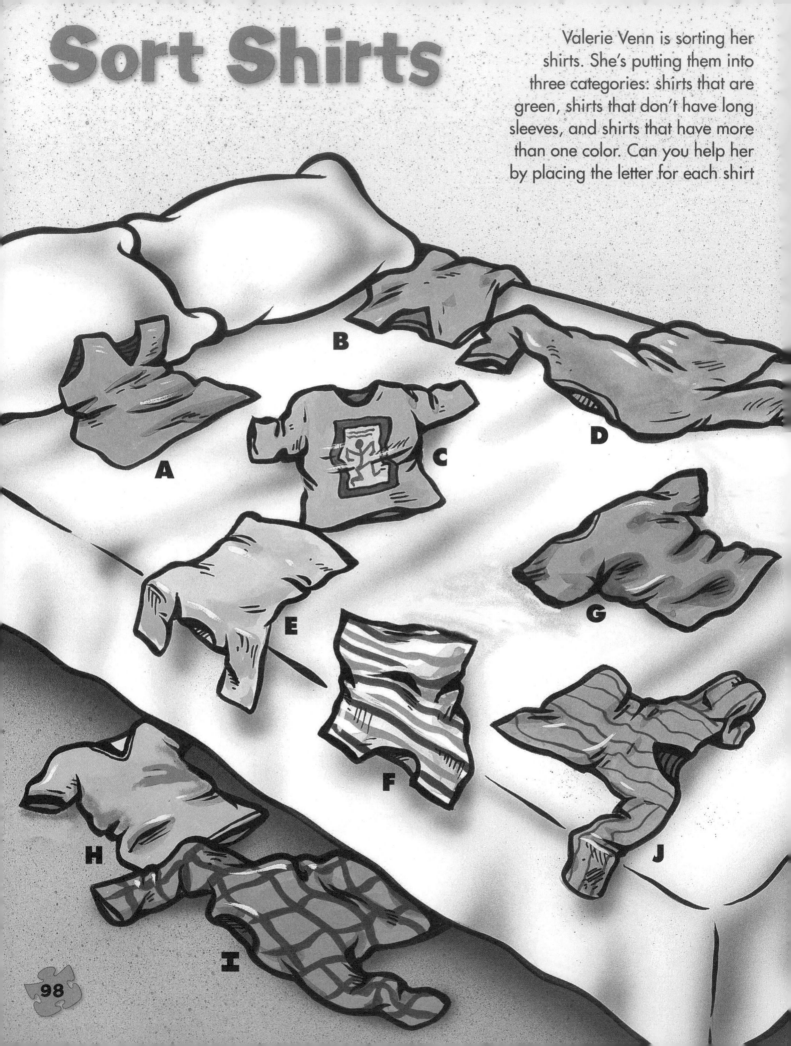

98

in the appropriate spot on her diagram at right?

Hint: Put the letter for a shirt that belongs in more than one category—a green shirt with short sleeves, for example—into the space where the circles overlap.

Shirts that don't have long sleeves

Shirts that have more than one color

Shirts that are green

Illustrated by Jerry Zimmerman

# If at First...

The answer to the riddle below is easy, if you know your measurements. Each "if" statement will give you a letter and tell you where to put it. Fill in all the letters and you will have your answer—no ifs, ands, or buts!

1. If a tablespoon is larger than a teaspoon, the first letter is a **C**. If not, it is a **D**.

2. If there are 36 inches in a yard, the second and ninth letters are **O**. If not, they are **A**.

3. If there are two pints in a quart, the tenth letter is a **U**. If not, the fifth letter is a **U**.

4. If there are 6,000 feet in a mile, letters 3, 4, and 8 are **T**. If not, they are **L**.

5. If there are 1,000 meters in a kilometer, letter 11 is an **R**. If not, it is an **S**.

6. If a millimeter is smaller than a centimeter, the sixth letter is an **E**. If not, it is an **R**.

7. If a ton is more than 1,000 pounds, the seventh letter is an **F**. If not, it is a **B**.

8. If a meter is longer than a foot, the fifth letter is an **I**. If not, the tenth letter is an **I**.

**What do you call dough used for making dog biscuits?**

___ ___ ___ ___ ___ ___ ___ ___ ___ ___ ___
1   2   3   4   5   6   7   8   9   10  11

Illustrated by Kelly Kennedy

# Wrong-Way Woolies

The Woolies are hat hunters. They will hike through any jungle or swim any ocean just to get the latest headgear. But they are bad with directions. From the clues below, can you figure out which island is home to the wild Woolies?

1. The Woolies' island does not have a volcano.
2. There is a stream on the Woolies' island.
3. There is no snow on their island.
4. The Woolies' island is not between any other islands.
5. There are no flowers on the Woolies' island.

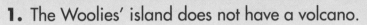

# Times Trail

To find your way through this maze, multiply the first pair of numbers **(5x5)**. Draw a line to the answer **(25)**, then move to the next pair of numbers and do the same. Answers may be to the left, right, up, or down.

Start

| 5x5 | 25 | 8x7 | 56 | 4x7 | 28 | 12x0 | 12 | 4x3 |
| 20 | | 42 | | 14 | | 0 | | 5 |
| 4x5 | 26 | 4x9 | 30 | 6x5 | 24 | 3x8 | 12 | 5x1 |
| 2 | | 36 | | 32 | | 27 | | 0 |
| 3x3 | 9 | 9x2 | 27 | 3x9 | 13 | 6x4 | 5 | 8x0 |
| 2 | | 18 | | 0 | | 24 | | 24 |
| 2x2 | 6 | 6x2 | 16 | 8x5 | 40 | 8x4 | 32 | 7x4 |
| 15 | | 12 | | 1 | | 36 | | 28 |
| 5x2 | 28 | 4x7 | 0 | 3x3 | 16 | 6x6 | 13 | 3x7 |
| 10 | | 24 | | 6 | | 49 | | 21 |
| 6x3 | 18 | 11x2 | 22 | 9x1 | 9 | 7x7 | 39 | Finish |

102

# BLOOMING 🌼 HUMOR

Flowers in the Puzzlemania garden do more than look pretty—they also crack codes! Count the number of petals on a flower. Then write the matching code letter in the center of the flower. Continue to fill in the flowers to find the answer to the riddle.

## KEY

| | |
|---|---|
| 3 - E | 9 - K |
| 4 - D | 10 - A |
| 5 - I | 11 - T |
| 6 - R | 12 - B |
| 7 - H | 13 - W |
| 8 - G | 14 - L |

**What did the dog do after he swallowed a firefly?**

H E

B A R K E D

W I T H

D E - L I G H T !

Illustrated by Jim Steck

# City Stops

Time's ticking! The bus driver has a busy schedule. Follow the maze to each stop on the bus's route, and follow the directions at each site to answer the riddle at the bottom.

## STOP 1:
Four people board the bus at the 4-Point Fountain. Put an **E** in the blank that matches the number of people now on board.

**4-POINT FOUNTAIN**

## START:
The bus driver has four passengers in the back. Put a **D** in the blank that matches the number of people on board. (Don't forget the bus driver!)

The RIGHT ANGLE RESTAURANT

## STOP 3:
Seven hungry people get off at the Right Angle Restaurant, and three people get on. The driver waits for two more people to board. Put a **T** in the correct blank.

## STOP 2:
Three people get off the bus at the Museum of Modern Math, and two hop on. Put an **A** in the correct blank.

**MUSEUM OF MODERN MATH**

## PYTHAGORAS PUBLIC LIBRARY

**STOP 5:**
Four book lovers depart at Pythagoras Public Library. Put an **O** in the correct blank.

**STOP 4:**
One person gets off at Prime Square, and two people with a lot of shopping bags board. Put an **H** in the correct blank.

**PRIME SQUARE**

**PERFECT PLUS PARK**

**FINISH:**
Last stop. All but one passenger leaves. Put an **R** in the correct blank. Have you answered the riddle?

Illustrated by Mike Dammer

**What runs through a city without ever moving?**

T H E   R O A D
6 7 9   2 3 8 5

# Flag Figures

Each triangle on these pages is worth 3 points. Each quadrilateral (a shape with 4 sides, such as a rectangle or a square) is worth 4 points. Can you match each flag with its total value, which is listed on the club box? Keep a sharp lookout. Look for shapes within other shapes, such as a small triangle that is part of a rectangle.

**COVER UP THIS CLUE BOX FOR AN EXTRA CHALLENGE!**

| FLAG VALUES | | | |
|---|---|---|---|
| 9 | 6 | 20 | 18 |
| 12 | 10 | 16 | 28 |

# Hidden Pictures
# Moose Math

light bulb

bowl

slice of bread

magnet

tweezers

ice pop

teacup

slice of cake

scissors

108

Illustrated by Diana Zourelias

caterpillar

glove

spoon

heart

candle

needle

butterfly

lollipop

ruler

wristwatch

toothbrush

# One, Zwei, Three

The numbers one through ten appear here in both English and German. Each will fit into the grid in only one way. Use the number of letters as a clue to where it might fit. We've filled in the first "one" to get you started. When you have filled the grid, write the shaded letters in order from top to bottom and left to right in the spaces below to see the German word for 100.
*Have fun! Viel spass!*

| ENGLISH | GERMAN |
| --- | --- |
| ~~One~~ | Eins |
| Two | Zwei |
| Three | Drei |
| Four | Vier |
| Five | Fünf |
| Six | Sechs |
| Seven | Sieben |
| Eight | Acht |
| Nine | Neun |
| Ten | Zehn |

**The German word**

**for 100 is:**

☐ ☐ ☐ ☐ ☐ ☐ ☐ ☐ ☐ .

# Tile Totals

It is a busy day for Dan's Tile Toters. Dan's workers will be putting down new tiles on five different patios in town. Can you figure out how many tiles they will need for each job?

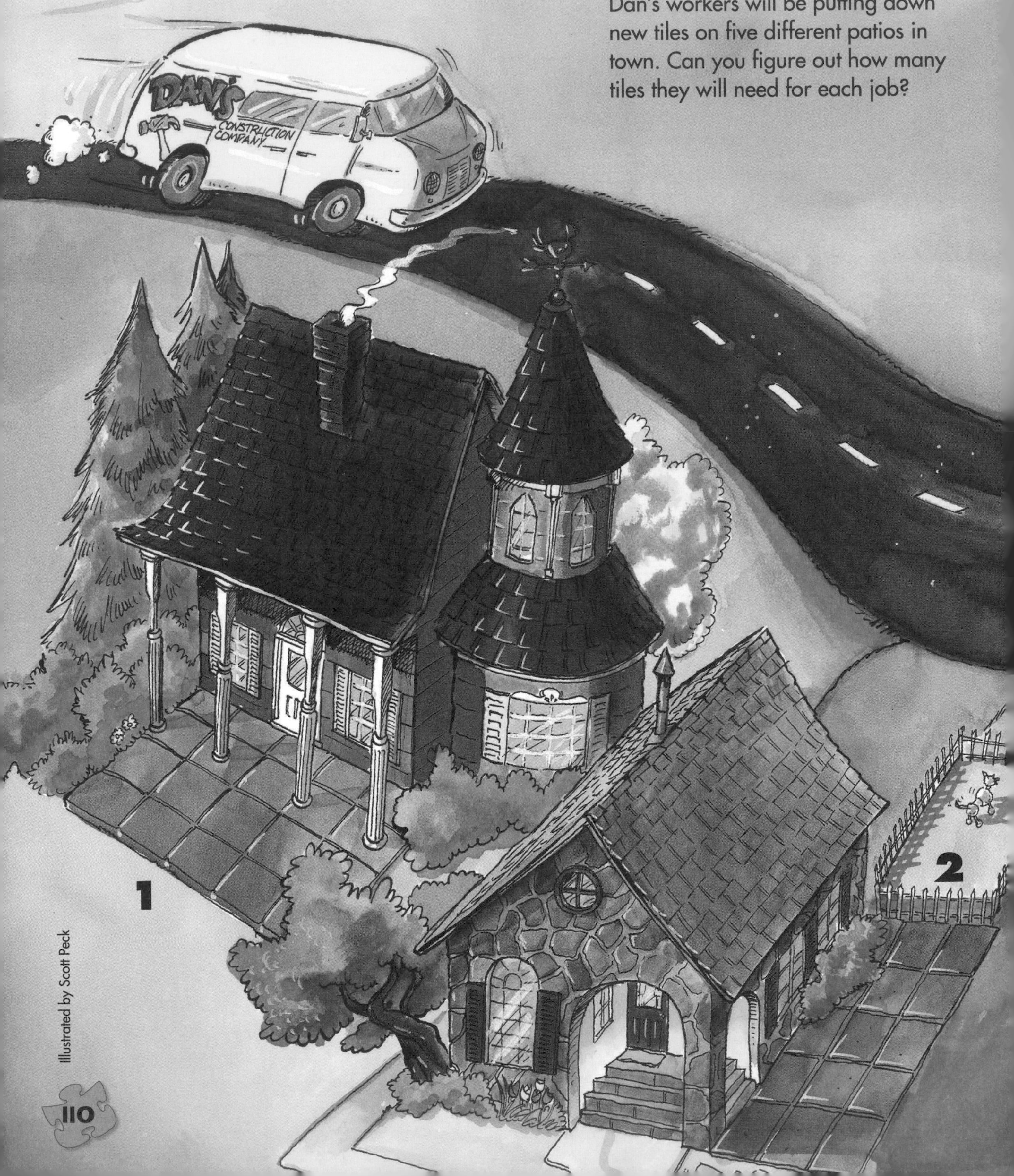

1

2

Remember, although some tiles may be hidden by trees and other objects, every patio is a rectangle. Can you also figure out how many tiles Dan will need in all?

5

4

3

ROGER

111

# Candy Counter

**SUPER CHALLENGE**

Clark has a dollar to spend. He will walk out of this store with 100 pieces of three different kinds of candy. Looking at the cost per piece of candy, can you tell how many pieces of each kind of candy will be in his bag?

**Licorice whips:**
10 cents

**Lollipops:**
3 cents

**Gum balls:**
2 for
1 cent

Illustrated by Terri Kovalcik

# Wonder Window

Illustrated by Jason Thorne

# Good Sports

At Puzzlemania, sports are more than just fun—they're also code crackers! Use the list of sports to solve the puzzle. Each coded space has two numbers. The first number tells you which sport to look at; the second number tells you which letter to use. For example, the first coded letter is 2–6. The 2 tells you to go to SQUASH. Count 6 letters in, and you've got an H.

# Sports List

1. HOCKEY
2. SQUASH
3. BASEBALL
4. FOOTBALL
5. SWIMMING
6. LACROSSE
7. BASKETBALL
8. GYMNASTICS
9. SNOWBOARDING

Why did the kangaroo lose the basketball game?

H E  R A
‾2-6 ‾3-4  ‾6-4 ‾4-6 ‾8-4  ‾4-2 ‾2-3 ‾7-6  ‾6-5 ‾4-1

‾7-7 ‾1-2 ‾2-3 ‾5-7 ‾9-9 ‾3-3 .

What kind of player gives refunds?

‾3-2  ‾2-2 ‾2-3 ‾7-2 ‾6-4 ‾4-4 ‾1-5 ‾6-4 ‾3-1 ‾6-2 ‾1-3 ‾7-4

What's the best thing to drink during a marathon?

‾6-4 ‾2-3 ‾9-2 ‾8-4 ‾5-3 ‾5-7 ‾8-1  ‾9-4 ‾7-2 ‾4-4 ‾1-5 ‾6-4

How is a baseball player like a songwriter?

‾7-1 ‾4-3 ‾8-7 ‾2-6  ‾5-2 ‾6-2 ‾9-2 ‾4-4  ‾3-1 ‾5-3 ‾8-1  ‾1-1 ‾9-10 ‾7-6  ‾2-1 .

# SHadoW Casting

Which shadow will be cast by these shapes?

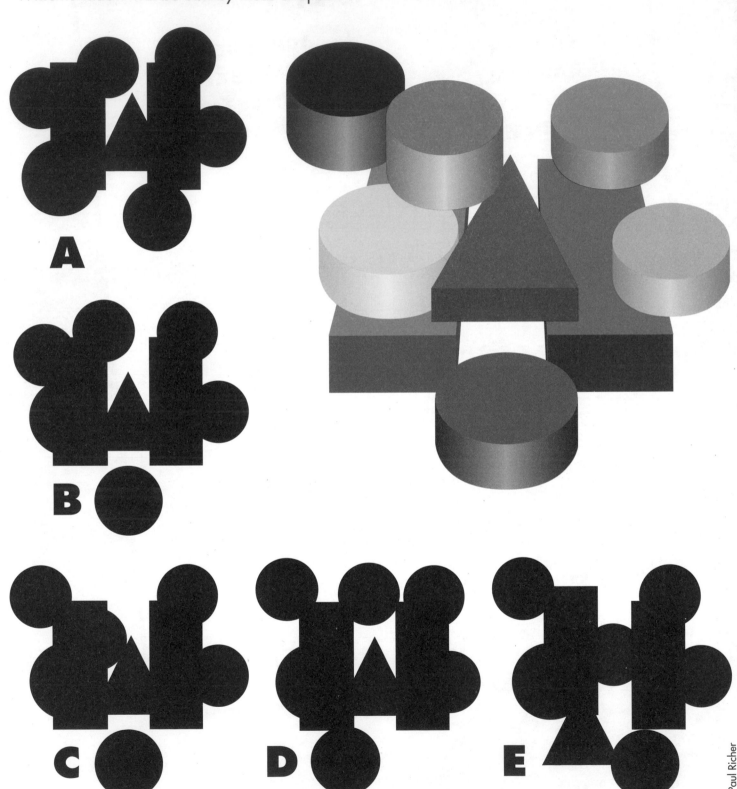

**A**

**B**

**C**

**D**

**E**

Illustrated by Paul Richer

# WHO SCREAMS FOR ICE CREAM?

Camila and her friends each ordered a treat at Isaac's Ice-Cream Parlor. But Isaac can't remember what they ordered! Using the clues below, can you figure out what ice-cream flavor each friend ordered and how they wanted it served?

Use the chart to keep track of your answers. Put an **X** in each box that can't be true and an **O** in boxes that match.

|  | Bowl | Sugar Cone | Shake | Waffle Cone | Peanut Butter | Cookies & Cream | Chocolate | Strawberry |
|---|---|---|---|---|---|---|---|---|
| **Camila** |  | O | X |  | X | O | O |  |
| **Oscar** |  |  |  |  | O |  |  |  |
| **Lilli** | O |  | X |  | X |  |  |  |
| **Daniel** |  |  |  |  | X |  | O |  |

1. A boy ordered a peanut-butter shake.
2. The flavor in Camila's sugar cone starts with the same letter as her name.
3. Lilli enjoyed her bowl of ice cream.
4. Daniel is allergic to nuts, but he likes chocolate.

Puzzle by Jenelle Woods

# Got a Minute?

There is no time like the present in Hickory's Clock Shop. Hickory sets his clocks to all different times, but there is a pattern.

118

The clocks are set in pairs with their times exactly three hours apart. See if you can find all the pairs of clocks before time runs out.

6:45

# Harvest Helpers

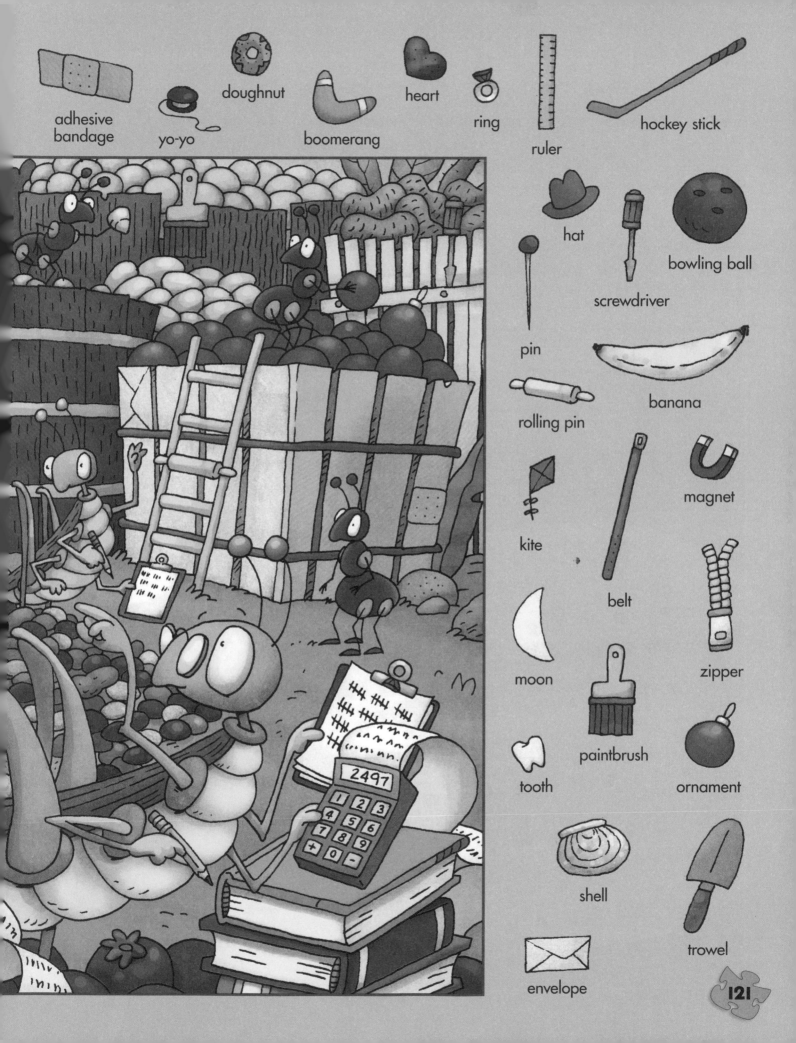

adhesive
bandage

yo-yo

doughnut

boomerang

heart

ring

ruler

hockey stick

hat

screwdriver

bowling ball

pin

banana

rolling pin

kite

belt

magnet

zipper

moon

paintbrush

tooth

ornament

shell

trowel

envelope

2497

121

# QWERTY Code

Here's a different "type" of puzzle. Use the keyboard to decode the answers to these riddles. For the first two riddles, change each letter to the one found on the **◀ LEFT** of it on the keyboard. For the last two riddles, change each letter to the one on the **RIGHT ▶** of it on the keyboard.

**1.** What do you call a computer superhero? Look 1 key **LEFT** on the keyboard.

A _ _ _ _ _ _ _ _ _
S   D V T R R M   D S B R T

**2.** Why did the computer cross the road? Look 1 key **LEFT** on the keyboard.

_ _ _ _ _ _ _ _ _ _ _ _ _
Y P   H R Y   S   N U Y R   Y P   R S Y

**3.** Why did the computer get glasses? Look 1 key **RIGHT** on the keyboard.

T _ _ _ _ _ _ _
R I   U N O E I C W

_ _ _ _ _ _ _ _ _
U R A   Q W V   A U F G R

**4.** Where do computers go to dance? Look 1 key **RIGHT** on the keyboard.

_ _ _ _ _ _ _ - _
R G W   S U A J   I

Puzzle by Anita Dualeh

# Venn Again

Find the answer to the riddle using the Venn diagram shown here. Look for the number described in each clue. Then match that number with the letter at the beginning of the clue. Write that letter in the blank above the matching number. The first one has been done to start you off.

Numbers in diagram: 1, 2, 3, 4, 5, 6, 7, 8, 9, 10, 11, 12

E — In the ▢, but in no other shape: __7__

O — In all the shapes except the ◯ : _____

A — In the △ and ◯, but not in the ▢ or ▱ : _____

Y — In the ▱, but in no other shape: _____

E — In none of the shapes: _____

W — In all the shapes except the ▱ : _____

T — In the △, but in no other shape: _____

L — In the △ and ▢, but not in the ◯ or ▱ : _____

D — In all four shapes: _____

S — In the △ and ▱, but not in the ◯ or ▢ : _____

R — In the ◯, but in no other shape: _____

G — In the △, ▱, and ◯, but not in the ▢ : _____

## What do fireflies say at the start of a race?

"_ _E_ _ _ _ _, _ _ _, _ _ _ _!"

3  7  4  8  12    11  2  1    10  6  9  5

Illustrated by Diana Zourelias

123

# Square 100

Illustrated by Joe Boddy

The kids are trying to figure out how to fill in the blanks of the grid that Kerri just drew. The numbers in each group of four adjacent squares must total 100. The same number may appear more than once.

Look at the smaller grid for an example. We've drawn colored squares around groups of four squares that add up to 100. See if you can fill in the big grid below. Hint: Start with the four squares at the bottom left-hand corner.

| 25 | 35 | 15 |
|----|----|----|
| 10 | 30 | 20 |
| 15 | 45 | 5  |

# Digit Does It!

That astounding investigator Inspector Digit has been called on to find out who broke into the Llewellyn Library and burgled some books. For a place that once held so many books, this spot has few clues. But wait! The inspector has found

a coded message. If you can decipher it, perhaps Digit will be able to recover the purloined paperbacks. The first line reads, "Dear Inspector Digit."

__ __ __ __    __ __ __ __ __ __ __ __ __ __    __ __ __ __ __ ,
8 10 2 15    16 21 13 17 10 6 11 19 15    8 16 1 16 11

__ __ __ __    __ __    __ __ __ __    __    __ __ __ __
11 2 18 10    22 5    3 19 15 8    16    19 21 20 5

__ __ __ __    __ __    __ __ __ __ __    __ __ __ __
3 2 21 11    11 19    4 19 15 15 19 3    13 19 22 10

__ __ __ __ __    __    __ __ __ __    __ __ __ __ __ __
4 19 19 18 13    16    3 16 20 20    15 10 11 9 15 21

__ __ __ __    __ __ __    __ __ __ __ __    __ __ __ .
11 14 10 22    3 14 10 21    16 22    8 19 21 10

__ __    __ __ __    __ __ __ __    __ __ __
16 12    5 19 9    12 16 21 8    11 14 10

__ __ __ __ __ __ __ __ __    __ __ __ __ __ __ __
21 16 21 10 11 10 10 21    7 19 20 9 22 10 13

__    __ __ __ __    __ __ __ __ __ __    __ __ __ __ __ __
16    20 10 12 11    4 10 14 16 21 8    17 20 10 2 13 10

__ __ __ __    __ __ __ __ __    __    __ __ __ __
1 16 7 10    11 14 10 22    2    1 19 19 8

__ __ __ __ __
13 14 10 20 12

__ __ __ __    __ __ __ __ __
15 16 11 2    13 11 19 15 5

# Light-Years Fantastic

The crew of the spaceship Tralfamawindo is in deep trouble. It has only enough energy pods left to travel 57 light-years. Can you add up the light-year distances to see which celestial body the crew can reach by going until the fuel dial reads exactly empty?

Illustrated by Scott Peck

129

# Different Strokes

Mason and his friends competed in the city swim meet. Each friend won first place in one race. Using the clues below, can you figure out what type of stroke and what distance each friend placed first in?

Use the chart to keep track of your answers. Put an **X** in each box that can't be true and an **O** in boxes that match.

| | Backstroke | Butterfly | Freestyle | Individual Medley | 50 Meters | 100 Meters | 200 Meters | 400 Meters |
|---|---|---|---|---|---|---|---|---|
| **Sarah** | | | | | | | | |
| **Will** | | | | | | | | |
| **Liz** | | | | | | | | |
| **Mason** | | | | | | | | |

1. The girls won races that start with the same letter.
2. Will's race was half the distance of Liz's.
3. The backstroke race was 100 meters long.
4. The race Sarah won was twice as long as Liz's.
5. A boy won the longest race, the individual medley.

130

# Hidden Pictures®
# Bridge Building

Illustrated by Chuck Dillon

penguin

pointy hat

snail

slice of pie

hammer

pennant

drinking
straw

spoon

candle

toothbrush

scrub
brush

ring

button

tack

131

# Box Out!

Follow the directions to cross out certain boxes. When you're done, write the remaining letters in order from left to right and top to bottom. They will give you the answer to the riddle.

**Cross out all numbers divisible by 4.**
**Cross out all numbers divisible by 5.**

| | | | | | |
|---|---|---|---|---|---|
| M ~~8~~ | A 11 | Y 40 | N 24 | N 17 | A 12 |
| O 19 | M 16 | C 23 | E 20 | C 15 | A 30 |
| L 32 | I 25 | F 4 | T 31 | O 10 | O 34 |
| R 45 | P 18 | D 5 | R 55 | X 28 | Y 44 |
| Z 35 | E 20 | U 38 | B 65 | T 25 | W 52 |
| S 22 | K 36 | N 48 | H 50 | N 60 | S 26 |

**What do you call a cat that has lost one of its nine lives?**

— — ___ — — — — - — — — —

Illustrated by Brian White

## 5 Leaping Lemurs

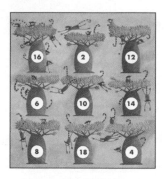

## 6–7 What's for Dessert?

What's the best thing to eat in a bathtub?
A SPONGE CAKE

Why do doughnuts go to the dentist?
TO GET FILLINGS

Who serves ice cream faster than a
speeding bullet? SCOOPERMAN!

Why did the baker stop making doughnuts?
HE GOT TIRED OF THE HOLE BUSINESS.

## 8–9 Shipshape Aquarium

## 10 Add It Up

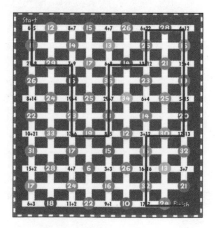

## 11 Order in the Court!

A.  29    Keep adding 7
B.  12    Keep subtracting 6
C.  4     Keep dividing by 2
D.  81    Keep multiplying by 3
E.  56    Keep adding 13
F.  54    Keep subtracting by 9
G.  4     Keep dividing by 4
H.  625   Keep multiplying by 5
I.  78    Write the numbers 1 through 8
          as two-digit numbers
J.  25    Numbers are the squares of
          1, 2, 3, 4, 5
K.  23    Numbers that have a 2 in
          ascending order
L.  18    Numbers go down 6 and then up 12
M.  56    Numbers in 1s place increase by 1
          Numbers in 10s place increase by 1
N.  66    Numbers made up only of 3s
          and 6s
O.  29    Add 5 and then subtract 3
P.  16    Multiply by 4 and then divide by 3
Q.  12    Subtract 3 and then add 6
R.  90    Divide by 4 then multiply by 6

## 12–13 Zero Money

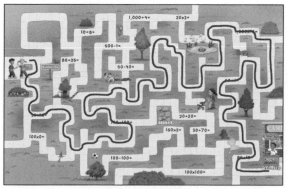

Nyle and Nadia collected 10 zeroes.
They can buy 5 lollipops.

# Answers

## 14–15 Ship Shapes

What does the ship weigh?
IT WEIGHS ANCHOR.

## 16 Thanksgiving Tidbits

The ingredients cost $10.75.

## 17 Pyramid Puzzles

```
            1
        3   3   6
      2   4   4   1   5
    7   4   1   1   3   1   5
 10   3   4   2   1   0   4   5  10
```

```
            9
        6   2   1
     29  17   8   2  10
   16   0   3   5   1  10  29
 30  14   1   4   6  26  10   1  30
```

```
               19
           16   6   5
        13  17   4  25  14
     18  23  18   7  15  28  16
   37  29  12   4  20   5  10  13  29
 59  22  12  11   4   3   9   7  30  30  59
```

## 18 Clock Comedy

Why was the clock so lonely?
IT HAD NO ONE TO TOCK TO.

## 19 One of a Kind

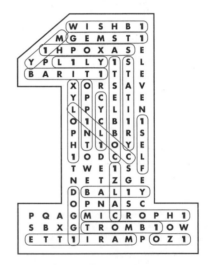

## 22 Five Sides

There are five flowers, squirrels, birds, ants (by the garbage can), and pieces of chalk (including the one in Fitz's hand).

## 20-21 Floral Arrangements

| A | B | C |
|---|---|---|
| $1.00 | $2.50 | $.50 |
| daisies | roses | carnations |

| D | E | F |
|---|---|---|
| $1.25 | $.75 | $2.00 |
| lilies | chrysanthemums | tulips |

## 23 Baking Day

## 26–27 Digit Does It

Dear Inspector Digit,

Please register these 23 stamps, which I trust you will return. When they are delivered to the court, another crook will be canceled.
Post Mark

## 28–29 Animal Airlift

The animals can be lifted out in four trips. Your order of trips may vary.

1. warthog, lion, okapi—
   130 + 550 + 300 = 980 pounds

2. hippopotamus, zebra, hyena—
   600 + 350 + 46 = 996 pounds

3. elephant, chimpanzee, meerkat, snake—
   800 + 95 + 20 + 80 = 995 pounds

4. giraffe, rhinoceros—
   325 + 675 = 1,000 pounds

(The weights given are only for these particular animals and do not represent the average weights of any species.)

## 31 Run for Fun

Rocky ran the race in 1 hour.
Rudy ran the race in 50 minutes.
Ronnie ran the race in 45 minutes.
Ronnie ran the fastest.

## 24–25 Ancient Auction

1. TRUE

2. TRUE

3. FALSE.

4. FALSE. This Stonian Museum has the winning bid on two items: the shoe and the necklace.

5. TRUE

6. FALSE. The Vannegie Institute is willing to spend the greatest sum of money— $142,060.

7. TRUE. If you subtract the lowest bid ($10,900) from the highest bid ($12,200), the difference is $1,300, the smallest difference of all the bids.

8. TRUE

What do you call a very, very, very old joke?
Pre-HYSTERIC

## 30 One, Dos, Three

The Spanish word for 100 is CIENTO.

## 32 Play by the Book

Rachel: mystery, skateboard
Eduardo: science fiction, bike
Abby: adventure, scooter
Daniel: humor, walking

# Answers

## 33 Hopscotch Game

## 36–37 Alley-Oops

When did the bowler like to practice?
IN HIS SPARE TIME

## 39 Don't Stair

| | | |
|---|---|---|
| 30 + 1 = 31 | 25 + 6 = 31 | 20 + 11 = 31 |
| 29 + 2 = 31 | 24 + 7 = 31 | 19 + 12 = 31 |
| 28 + 3 = 31 | 23 + 8 = 31 | 18 + 13 = 31 |
| 27 + 4 = 31 | 22 + 9 = 31 | 17 + 14 = 31 |
| 26 + 5 = 31 | 21 + 10 = 31 | 16 + 15 = 31 |

15 x 31 = 465 PIGEONS

## 40 For a Change

Miss Ellis: 705 coins; $20.00

Mrs. Macy: 531 coins; $18.30

Mr. Ryan: 725 coins; $19.34

Mr. Ryan's class collected the most coins, and Miss Ellis's class collected the most money.

## 42–43 Seaside Shapes

We found 31 triangles and 42 rectangles.
How many did you find?

## 45 To the Hoop

Player #8 scored 2 three-point baskets, 2 baskets, and 1 free throw.

## 34–35 Witch Way

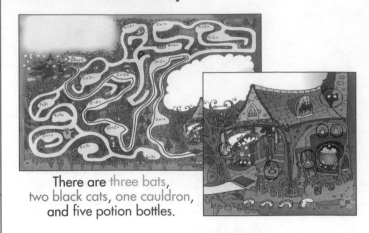

There are three bats, two black cats, one cauldron, and five potion bottles.

What do you call two witches who live together?
BROOMMATES

## 38 Party Path

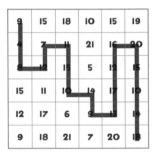

## 41 Totally!

1. 30 ÷ 3 = 10
   10 + 8 = 18
   18 − 4 = 14

3. 50 ÷ 2 = 25
   25 + 10 = 35
   35 − 24 = 11

2. **5 x 5 = 25**
   **25 + 20 = 45**
   **45 ÷ 3 = 15**

The name of Gidget's hamster is WIDGET.

## 44 Roaming Rover

Rover has found the dog bone.

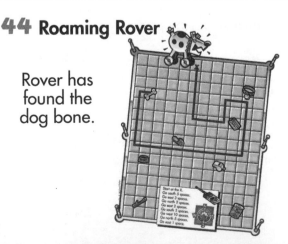

## 46 Clock Cleaning

## 47 The Key to It All

Gold: Car
Blue: Front
Red: Office
Green: Back
Purple: Shed

## 48–49 Watch the Difference

| 5:15—5:55 | 40 minutes | L |
|---|---|---|
| 4:55—5:45 | 50 minutes | O |
| 9:00—10:00 | 60 minutes | O |
| 7:35—9:00 | 1 hour, 25 minutes | K |
| 12:30—2:00 | 1 hour, 30 minutes | M |
| 6:00—8:30 | 2 hours, 30 minutes | A |
| 2:45—5:30 | 2 hours, 45 minutes | N |

| 3:00—6:00 | 3 hours | O |
|---|---|---|
| 2:40—5:50 | 3 hours, 10 minutes | H |
| 8:00—11:30 | 3 hours, 30 minutes | A |
| 7:00—10:45 | 3 hours, 45 minutes | N |
| 3:45—9:00 | 5 hours, 15 minutes | D |
| 1:00—10:00 | 9 hours | S |

What did the digital clock say to its mother?
"LOOK, MA! NO HANDS!"

## 50 Ice-Cream Dreams

Josh's ice cream cost $4.20.
Sammy started with $7.90.
Michaela and Neal gave Izzy $10.00.

## 52 Pattern Partners

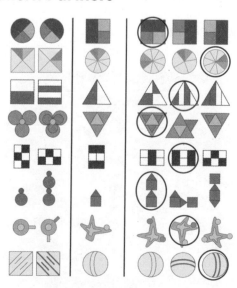

## 51 Zig Zag Zig

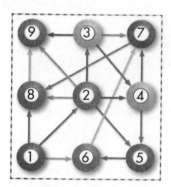

## 53 The King Wins

137

# Answers

## 54–55 Shell Search

Lola picked up 17 seashells, the most of anyone. Ashton picked up 15, Aimee 13, and Cameron 14.

## 58–59 Nothing To It

## 62 A Dirty Job

It will take Peter 16 trips to remove the entire pile.

(2,000 x 6 = 12,000 pounds; 12,000 ÷ 750 = 16)

## 64 Professor Parrot

## 56 Truck Tunes

What do long-distance truckers listen to?
CROSS-COUNTRY MUSIC

## 57 Minus Maze

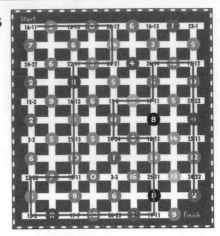

## 60–61 Folding Fun

1. G
2. H
3. E
4. B
5. C
6. D
7. F
8. A

## 63 Batting Logic

1. Cody
2. Hector
3. Claudia
4. Seth
5. Jacob
6. Ariel
7. Troy
8. Lindsey
9. Laura

## 65 Magic Maze

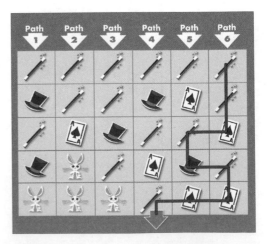

## 66–67 Hands Off

The clockmaker's name is NICK O'TIME.

## 70 Similar Circles

All the circles but one have 8 sections.
D has 9 sections.

## 72 Three's a Crowd

Where did the Three Musketeers
go on vacation?
THE BERMUDA TRIANGLE

## 73 Gone Fishing

Brooke: yellow, castle   Corinne: black, coral
Jon: blue, ship   Ethan: orange, mermaid

## 75 Piggy Problems

## 68 Toys for Twins

Nate and Jada bought the airplane, paints, puzzle, and dump truck for $13.20.

## 69 Going Up!

Here is our answer. You may have found another.

| 9 | 11 | 13 |
|---|----|----|
| 1 | 7 | 5 |
| 4 | 15 | 3 |
| 2 | 8 | 6 |
| 14 | 12 | 10 |

## 71 A Head For Figures

The number 61019 is the same when you turn it upside down.

## 74 Winning Number

Runner 25 won the race.

## 76–77 Jungle Fun

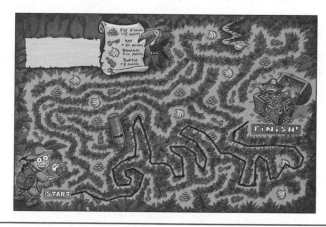

## 78–79 Money Maker

| 1 | 2 | 3 | 4 | 5 | 6 | 7 | 8 | 9 | 10 |
|---|---|---|---|---|---|---|---|---|----|
| 11 | 12 | 13 | 14 | 15 | 16 | 17 | 18 | 19 | 20 |
| 21 | 22 | 23 | 24 | 25 | 26 | 27 | 28 | 29 | 30 |
| 31 | 32 | 33 | 34 | 35 | 36 | 37 | 38 | 39 | 40 |
| 41 | 42 | 43 | 44 | 45 | 46 | 47 | 48 | 49 | 50 |
| 51 | 52 | 53 | 54 | 55 | 56 | 57 | 58 | 59 | 60 |
| 61 | 62 | 63 | 64 | 65 | 66 | 67 | 68 | 69 | 70 |
| 71 | 72 | 73 | 74 | 75 | 76 | 77 | 78 | 79 | 80 |
| 81 | 82 | 83 | 84 | 85 | 86 | 87 | 88 | 89 | 90 |
| 91 | 92 | 93 | 94 | 95 | 96 | 97 | 98 | 99 | 100 |

# Answers

## 80 Lucky Pyramid

## 81 Albert Einstein

## 82 One, Deux, Three

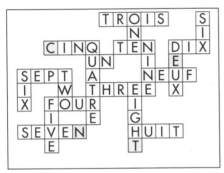

The French word for 100 is CENT.

## 83 For Good Measure

One solution begins with loading up the 3-ton truck and then dumping the 3 tons into the 5-ton truck. Load the 3-ton truck again, and again pour as much as you can into the 5-ton truck. The 5-ton truck will be able to hold only 2 more tons now, so 1 ton will stay in the smaller truck. Dump that 1 ton into the train car. Now load up the 3-ton truck and dump that load into the car.

## 84 Game On!

Andrew: Golf Guru, 2nd
Briana: Race Car Fun, 4th
Cassie: Zany Zoo, 1st
Diego: Space Traveler, 3rd

## 85 Math Mirth

What is a math teacher's favorite dessert?
PUMPKIN PI

Which knight helped King Arthur
build his round table?
SIR CUMFERENCE

## 86–87 Digit Does It!

Dear Inspector Digit,

Sorry to ring and run. I have Big Bill, the biggest bell in the collection, but I've left plenty behind. If you count the other bells, you'll know what room to ring me up in at the Belvedere Hotel.

## 88 Treasure Hunt

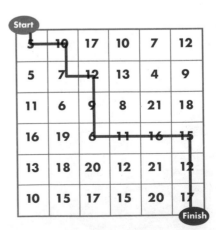

# Answers

## 89 Diamondbacks

## 90 Tricky Sticks

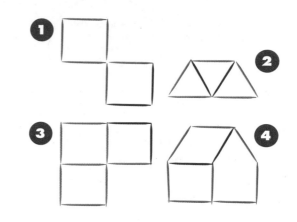

## 91 Owlgebra

## 92 Show Time

Lena: action, popcorn
Jack: comedy, taffy
Ethan: drama, chocolate bar
Jasmine: science fiction, licorice

## 93 Block Party

A. 3  B. 2  C. 1  D. 4

## 94–95 Knock Three Times

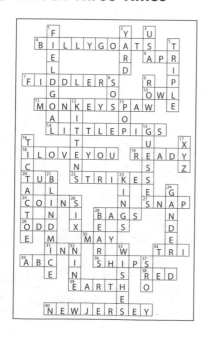

## 96 Choosing Chores

Jared made $6.50,
which is enough to buy the game.
Emilee has to take out the trash 3 times.

## 97 Pennant Winners

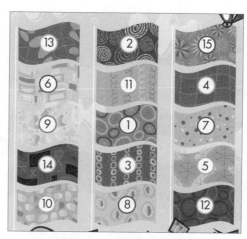

This is our answer.
You may have found another.

141

# Answers

## 98–99 Sort Shirts

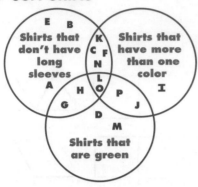

## 100 If at First . . .

What do you call dough used for making dog biscuits?

COLLIE FLOUR

## 101 Wrong-Way Woolies

## 102 Times Trail

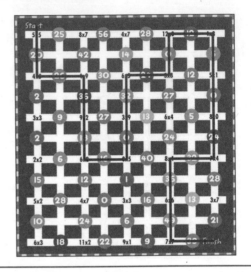

## 103 Blooming Humor

What did the dog do after he swallowed a firefly?

HE BARKED WITH DE-LIGHT!

## 104–105 City Stops

What runs through a city without ever moving?

THE ROAD

## 106–107 Flag Figures

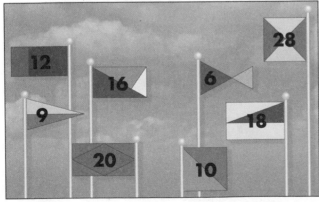

## 108 Moose Math

# Answers

## 109 One, Zwei, Three

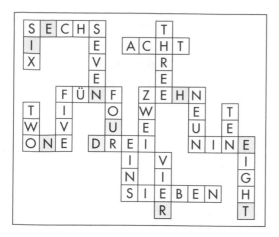

EIN HUNDERT is 100 in German.

## 112 Candy Counter

5 whips at 10 cents = .50
1 lollipop at 3 cents = .03
94 gum balls at 2 for 1 cent = .47

## 114–115 Good Sports

Why did the kangaroo lose the
basketball game?
HE RAN OUT OF BOUNDS.

What kind of player gives refunds?
A QUARTERBACK

What's the best thing to drink during
a marathon?
RUNNING WATER

How is a baseball player like a songwriter?
BOTH WANT BIG HITS.

## 117 Who Screams for Ice Cream?

Camila: Cookies-and-cream sugar cone
Oscar: Peanut-butter shake
Lilli: Strawberry bowl
Daniel: Chocolate waffle cone

## 110–111 Tile Totals

House 1: 5 tiles x 4 tiles = 20 tiles
House 2: 3 tiles x 5 tiles = 15 tiles
House 3: 8 tiles x 5 tiles = 40 tiles
House 4: 10 tiles x 4 tiles = 40 tiles
House 5: 7 tiles x 4 tiles = 28 tiles

Dan will need 143 tiles in all.

## 113 Wonder Window

There are more triangles.
We found more than 100 triangles
and fewer than 100 squares.
How many did you find?

## 116 Shadow Casting

Answer C is the correct shadow.

## 118–119 Got a Minute?

# Answers

## 120–121 Harvest Helpers

## 122 QWERTY Code

What do you call a computer superhero?
**A SCREEN SAVER**

Why did the computer cross the road?
**TO GET A BYTE TO EAT**

Why did the computer get glasses?
**TO IMPROVE ITS WEB SIGHT**

Where do computers go to dance?
**THE DISK-O**

## 123 Venn Again

| | | |
|---|---|---|
| E. 7 | E. 2 | D. 8 |
| O. 9 | W. 5 | S. 11 |
| A. 4 | T. 1 | R. 3 |
| Y. 12 | L. 6 | G. 10 |

What do fireflies say at the start of a race?
**"READY, SET, GLOW!"**

## 124–125 Square 100

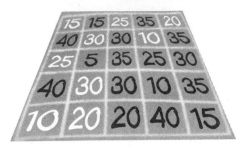

## 128–129 Light-Years Fantastic

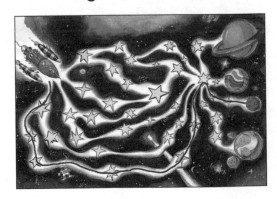

## 126–127 Digit Does It!

Dear Inspector Digit,

Take my word. I only want to borrow some books. I will return them when I'm done. If you find the nineteen volumes I left behind, please give them a good shelf.

Rita Story

## 130 Different Strokes

Sarah: Butterfly, 200 meters
Will: Freestyle, 50 meters
Liz: Backstroke, 100 meters
Mason: Individual Medley, 400 meters

## 131 Bridge Building

## 132 Box Out!

What do you call a cat that has lost one of its nine lives?
**AN OCTO-PUSS**